Uxbridge Ontario Book 2 in Colour Photos, Saving Our History One Photo at a Time

Photography by Barbara Raué
©2018

Series Name: Cruising Ontario

Book 219: Uxbridge Book 2

Cover photo: 39 Main Street North, Page 40

©All the photos in this book have been taken with my cameras. I own the rights to them.

Series Name: Cruising Ontario
Saving Our History One Photo at a Time
in colour photos

Books Available in Alphabetical Order:
Aberfoyle, Acton, Ajax, Alton, Amherstburg, Ancaster, Arthur, Auburn, Aylmer, Ayr, Beaver Valley, Belgrave, Belleville, Bloomingdale, Blyth, Brantford, Brockville, Burford, Burlington, Caledon, Caledonia, Cambridge, Carlow, Chatsworth, Clifford, Collingwood, Conestogo, Delhi, Dorchester to Aylmer, Drayton, Drumbo, Dundas, Dunlop, Eden Mills, Elmira, Elora, Erin, Essex, Fergus, Goderich, Grimsby, Guelph, Hagersville, Hamilton, Hanover, Harriston, Hespeler, Jarvis, Kingston, Kingsville, Kitchener, Lake Superior, Lincoln, Linwood, Listowel, London, Lucknow, Merrickville, Mono, Mount Forest, Mount Pleasant, Neustadt, New Hamburg, Newboro, Newport, Niagara-on-the-Lake, Niagara Falls, North Bay, Oakville, Onondaga, Orangeville, Orillia, Oshawa, Owen Sound, Palmerston, Paris, Pelham, Perth, Peterborough, Petrolia, Pickering, Port Colborne, Port Elgin, Portland, Preston, Rockwood, Sarnia, Sault Ste. Marie, Seaforth, Sheffield, Shelburne, Simcoe, Smiths Falls, Smithville, Southampton, St. Catharines, St. George, St. Jacobs, St. Marys, St. Thomas, Stoney Creek, Stratford, Thamesford, Thunder Bay, Tillsonburg, Toronto, Waterdown, Waterford, Waterloo, Welland, Wellesley, West Flamborough, Westport, Whitby, Windsor, Wingham, Woodstock

Book 201-202: Whitby
Book 203: Ajax, Pickering
Book 204-206: Oshawa
Book 207-209: Niagara Falls
Book 210: North Bay
Book 211: Fort Erie

Book 212-215 Haldimand County
Book 216: Sudbury
Book 217: Parry Sound
Book 218-219: Uxbridge

Table of Contents

Victoria Drive	Page 5
Church Street	Page 11
Mill Street	Page 17
Planks Lane	Page 19
East Street	Page 23
Marietta Street	Page 24
Main Street South	Page 25
Main Street North	Page 36
Franklin Street	Page 39
Reach Street	Page 43
Cedar Street North	Page 46
Maple Street	Page 50
King Street West	Page 50
Sandy Hook Road	Page 52
Regional Road 1	Page 53
Concession 6	Page 54
Leaskdale	Page 60
Goodwood	Page 63

Uxbridge is a township in the Regional Municipality of Durham in south-central Ontario and is located about forty kilometers northeast of Metropolitan Toronto. The main center in the township is the community of Uxbridge. Other communities within the township include Coppins Corners, Goodwood, Leaskdale, Sandford, Siloam, Victoria's Corner, and Zephyr.

It was named for Uxbridge, England, a name which was derived from "Wixan's Bridge".

The Uxbridge Historical Centre (UHC), established in 1972, has ten buildings on a five acre site overlooking the beautiful Uxbridge Valley and Oak Ridges Moraine. The life of the early settler comes alive at the Centre. Quaker pioneers first arrived in the area in the early 1800s. Millers, farmers, carpenters and others soon followed. Locally-made agricultural equipment, machinery, tools, and vehicles, as well as pianos, organs and other musical instruments are a few examples of the Centre's varied collection of artifacts.

With the creation of the Regional Municipality of Durham in 1974, Uxbridge Township was amalgamated with the Town of Uxbridge and Scott Township to create an expanded Township of Uxbridge.

Today, Uxbridge is mostly a suburban community in northern Durham Region. Major manufacturing employers include Pine Valley Packaging (packaging, containers and portable shelters), Koch-Glitsch Canada (mass transfer systems) and Hela Canada (spice and ingredient manufacture). Many residents commute to other centers in Durham and York Regions and beyond.

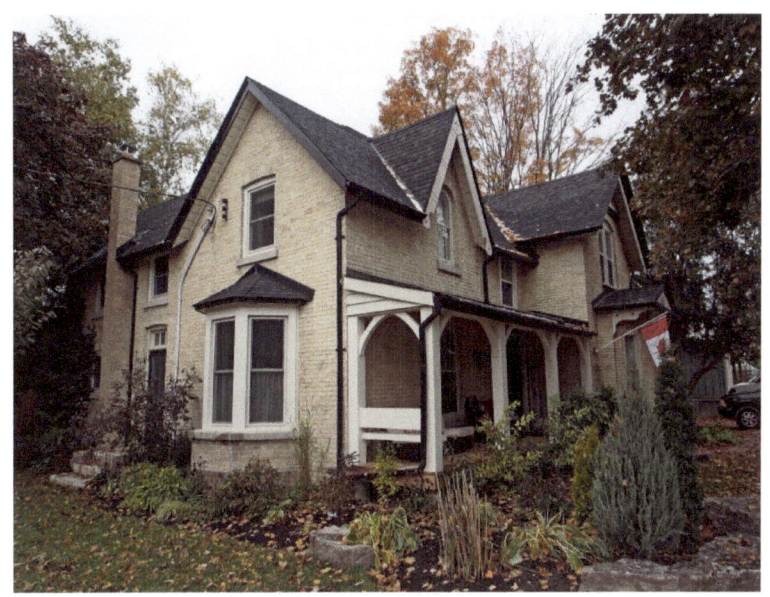

50 Victoria Drive

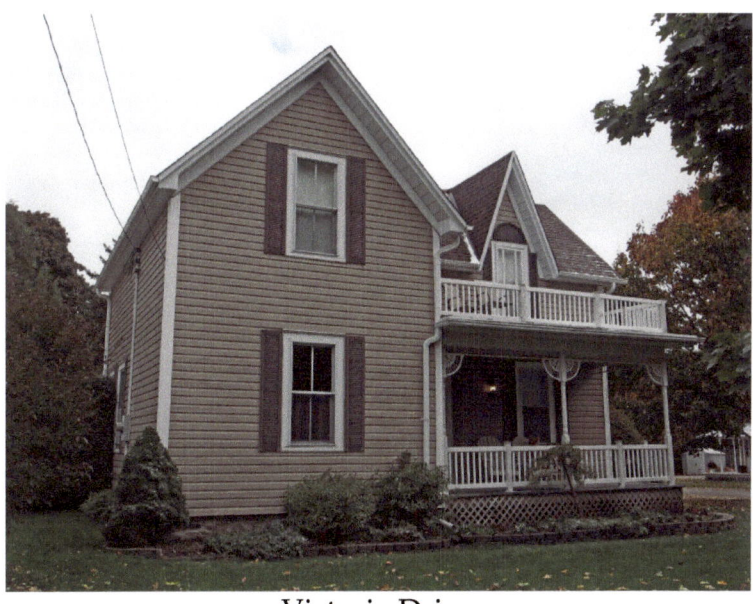

Victoria Drive

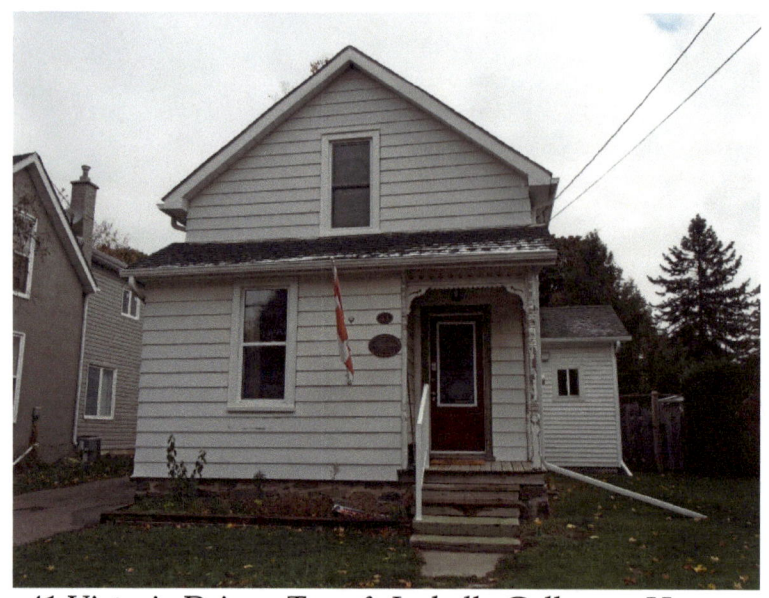

41 Victoria Drive - Tom & Isabella Galloway House, Theologian (1892-1906) – c. 1874

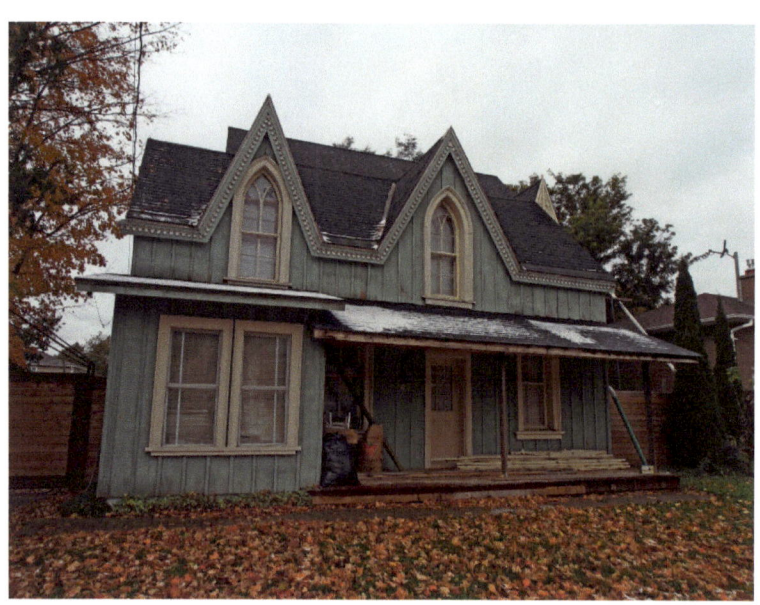

42 Victoria Drive - Gothic

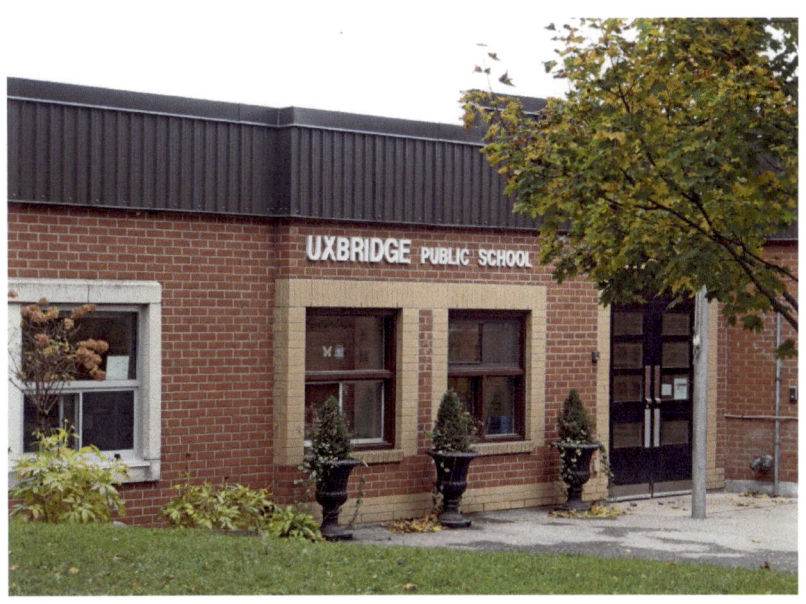

64 Victoria Drive – Uxbridge Public School, Site of School since 1873

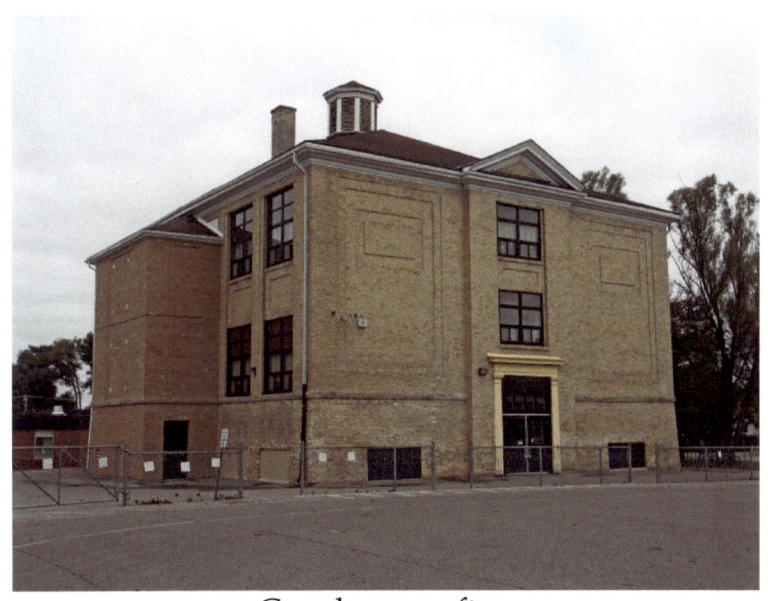

Cupola on rooftop

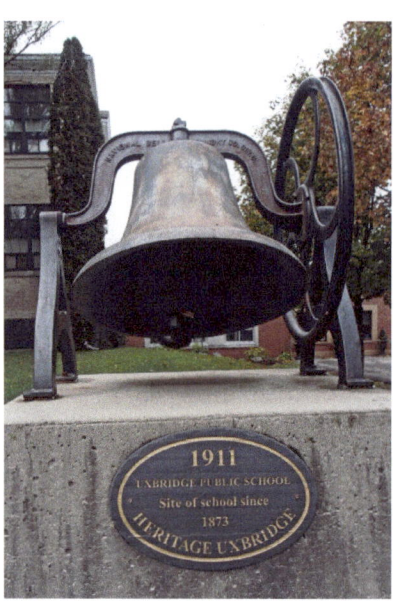

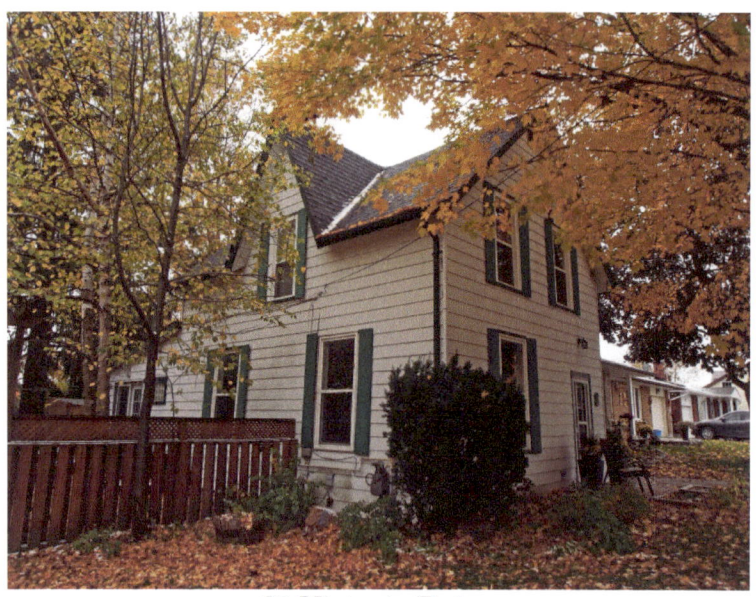

81 Victoria Drive

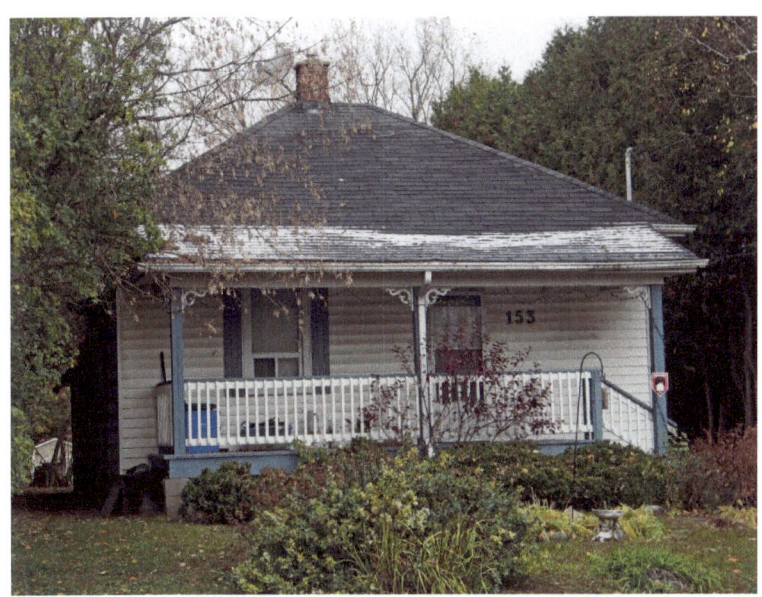

153 Victoria Drive – hipped roof

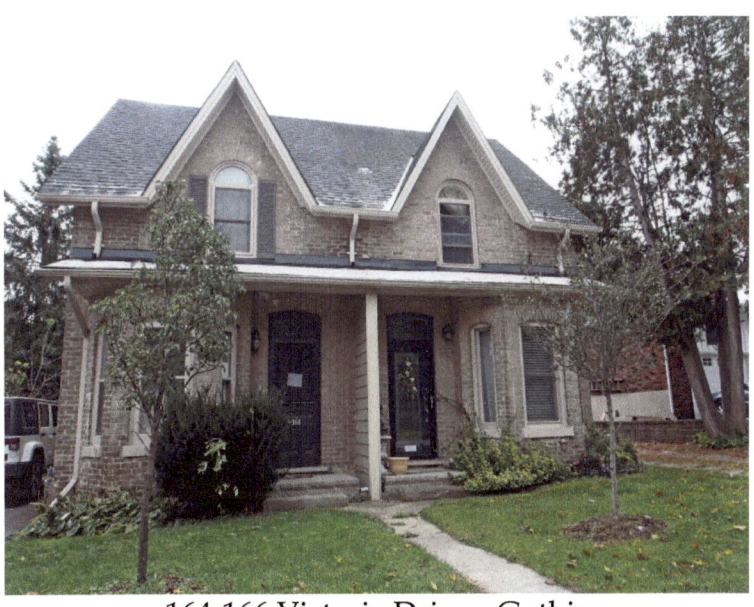

164-166 Victoria Drive - Gothic

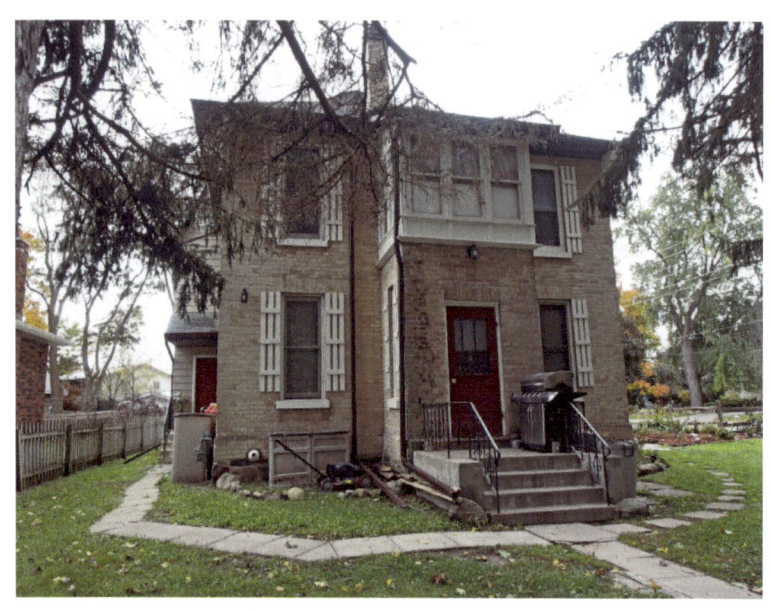

176 Victoria Drive

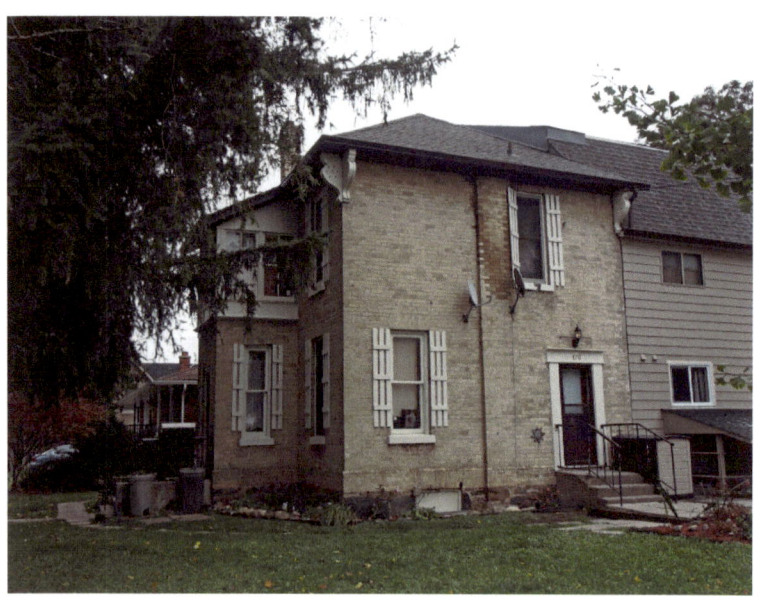

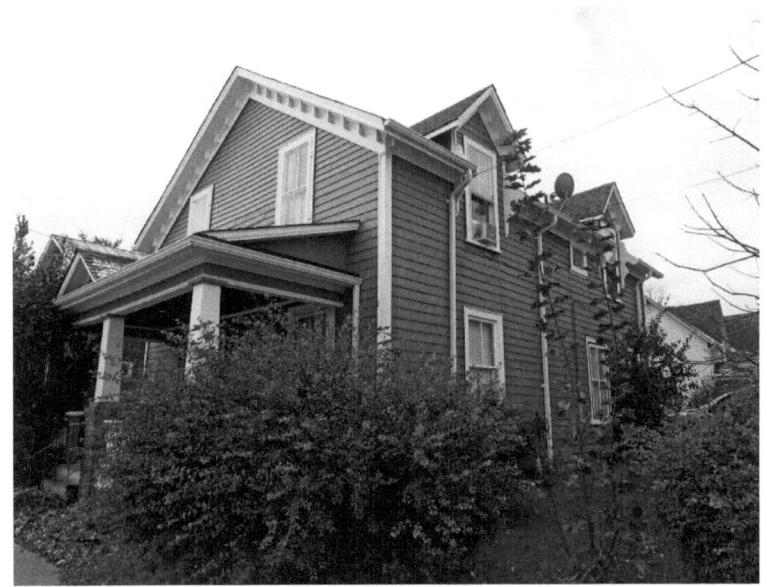

Church Street

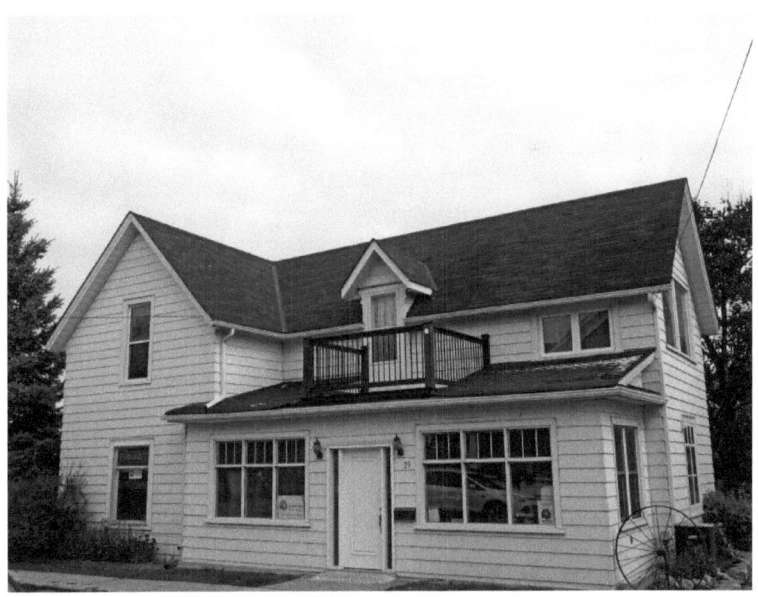

23 Church Street

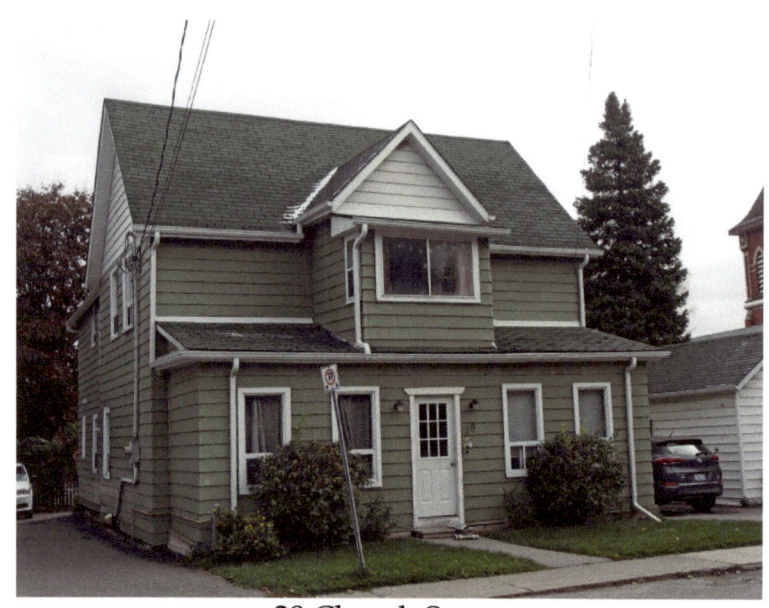

29 Church Street

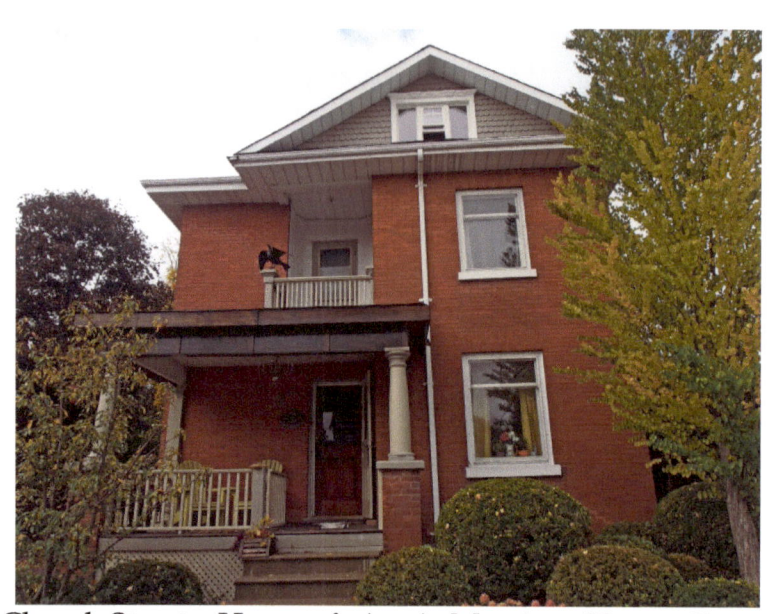

30 Church Street – Horace & Annie Morrison House, Farmer – c. 1911

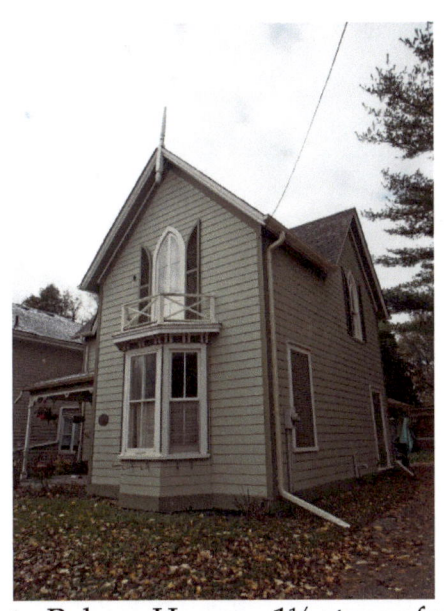

38 Church Street - Raham House – 1½ storey frame house built in 1871 with large and small gables and gothic style windows and an oriel window. It was purchased in 1896 by Joseph and Agnes Raham. Mr. Raham operated a carriage factory. Property was then sold to Jane Wilson who was a Councilor in 1897-98 and Reeve in 1911-12.

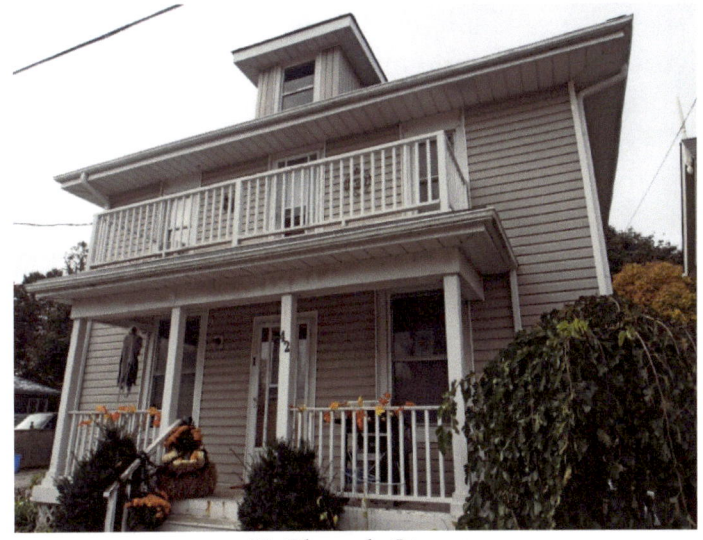

42 Church Street

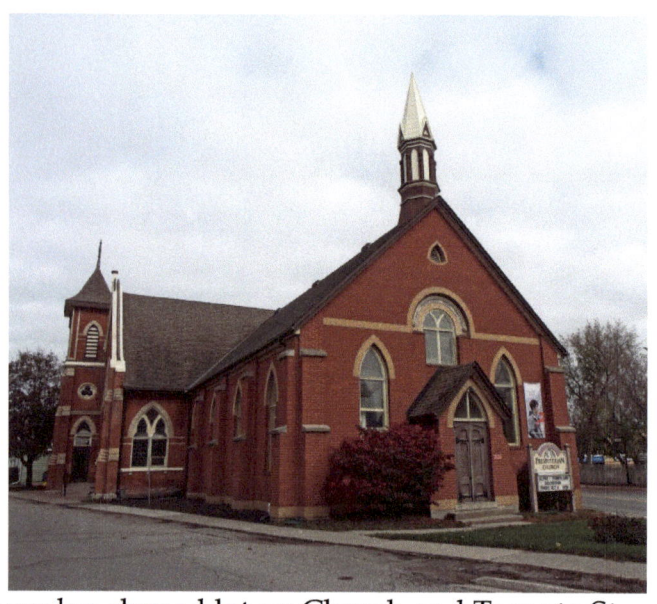

On this wedge-shaped lot on Church and Toronto Street South, St. Andrews-Chalmers Presbyterian Church presents an intriguing sight. A contemporary brick "skin" has been laid over the original structure while the date that is visible over the door is of the building hidden beneath. Period detail can be seen in the two wings (1884) projecting from either side of the church. Compare the contrasting color and texture of the bricks, and the use of the bricks themselves as decorative elements in the "new" and old areas.

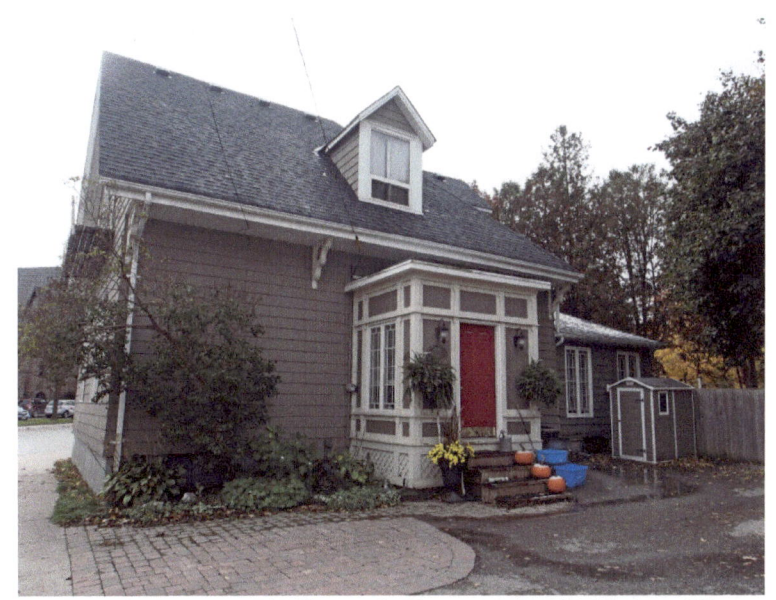

48 Church Street - William & Emma Finch-Henry House,
Clothing Merchant (1874-1934) – c. 1872

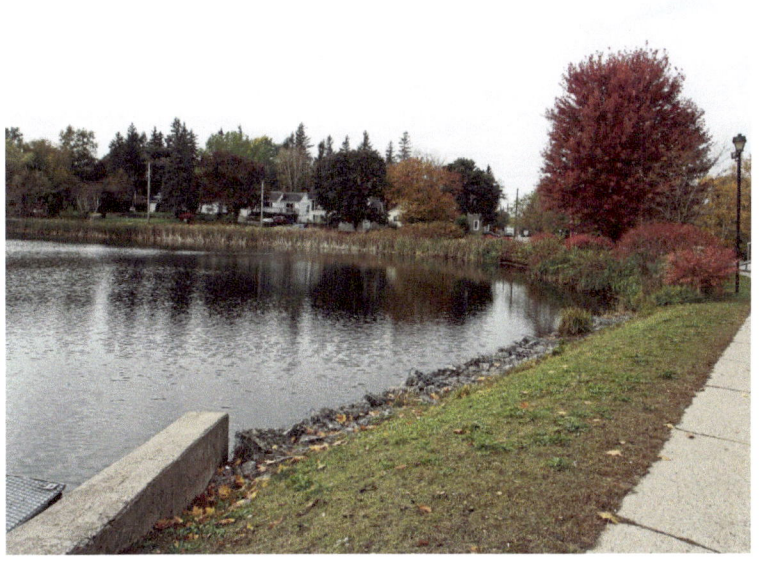

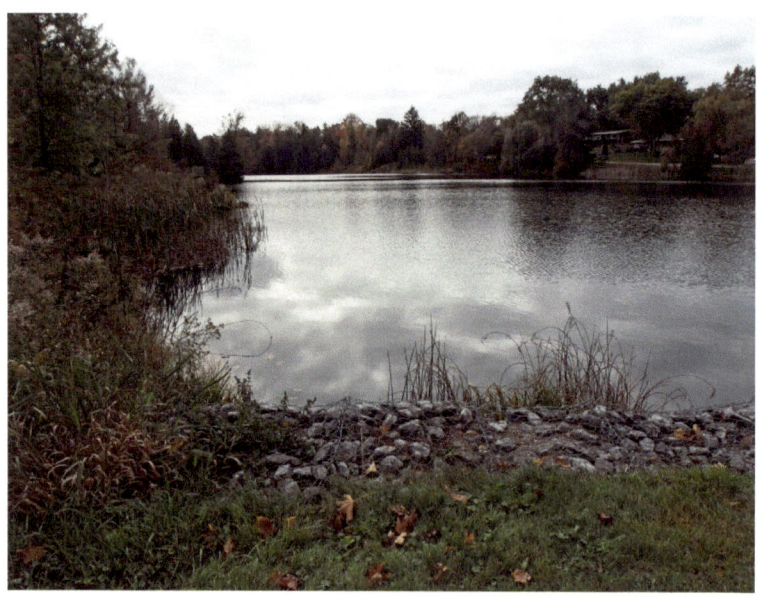

The Uxbridge Brook provided a steady supply of running water, and Joseph Gould, and later his son, dammed the brook to create ponds which acted as reservoirs to provide water-power for their mills. These ponds (Elgin Pond, the Electric Light Pond and the Mill Pond) were essential sources of power to drive the water wheels which in turn operated the machinery in the saw mill, the grist mills, and the carding (woolen) mill.

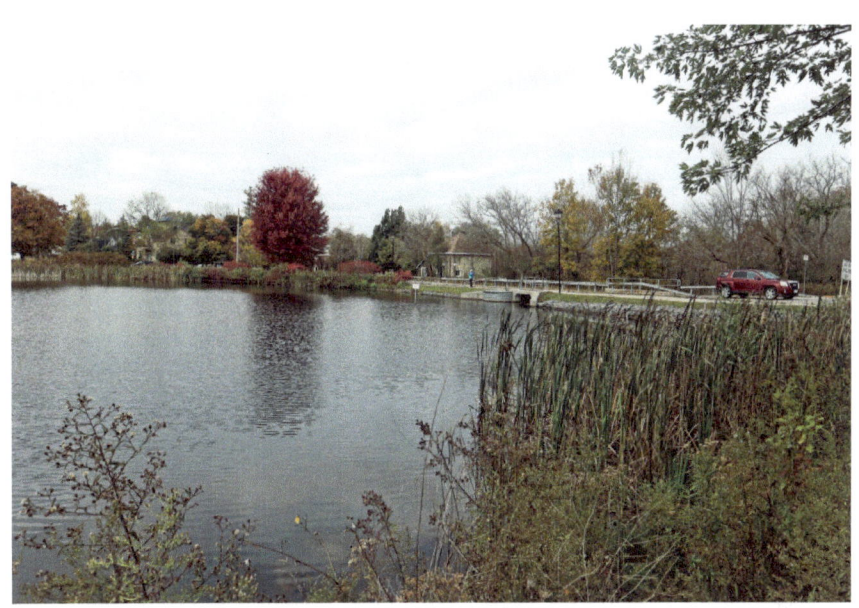

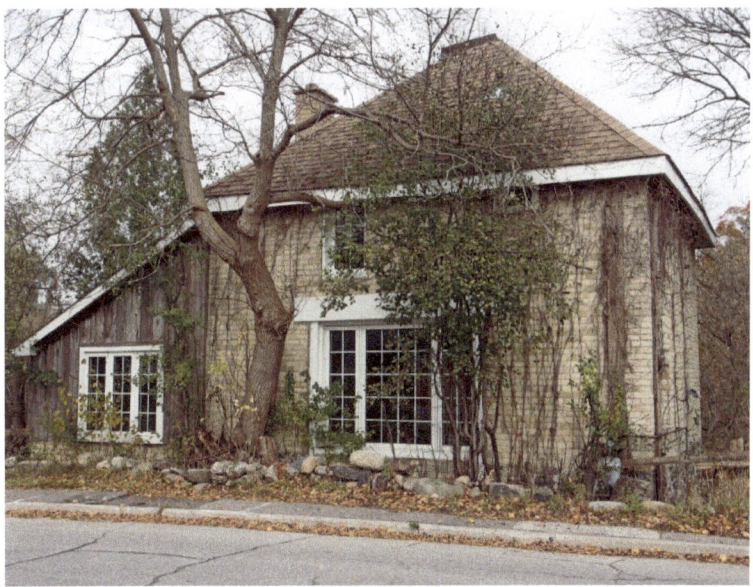

The oat mill on Mill Street was one of the largest buildings in town. It was built in 1886 and was demolished in 1957 after part of it collapsed. This small building at 11 Mill Street was the Isaac J. Gould Oatmeal Kiln for drying the grain. It is now a private residence.

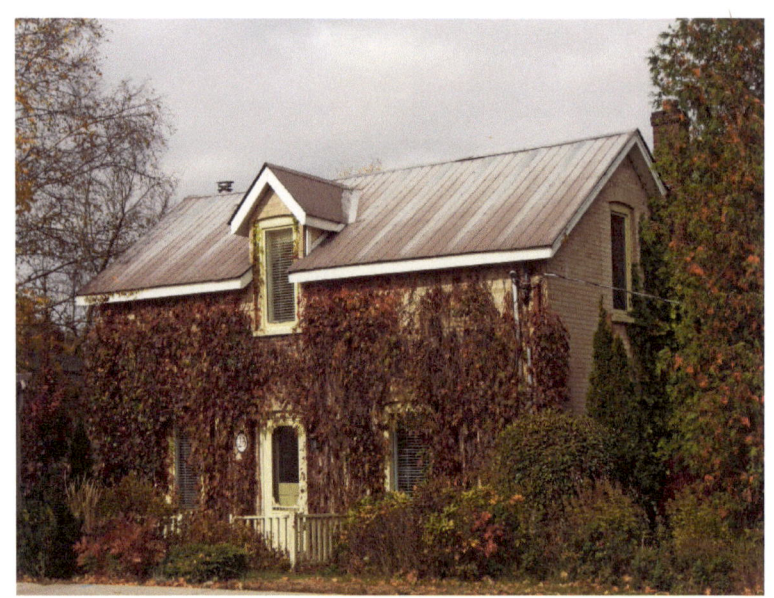

23 Mill Street

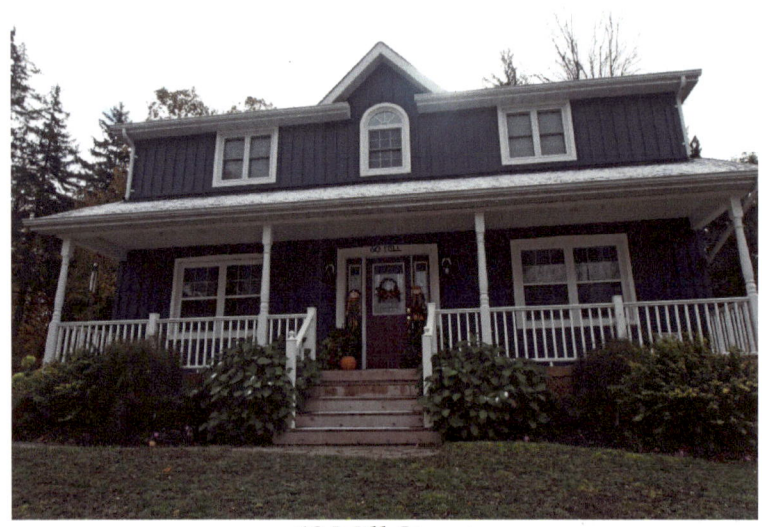

60 Mill Street

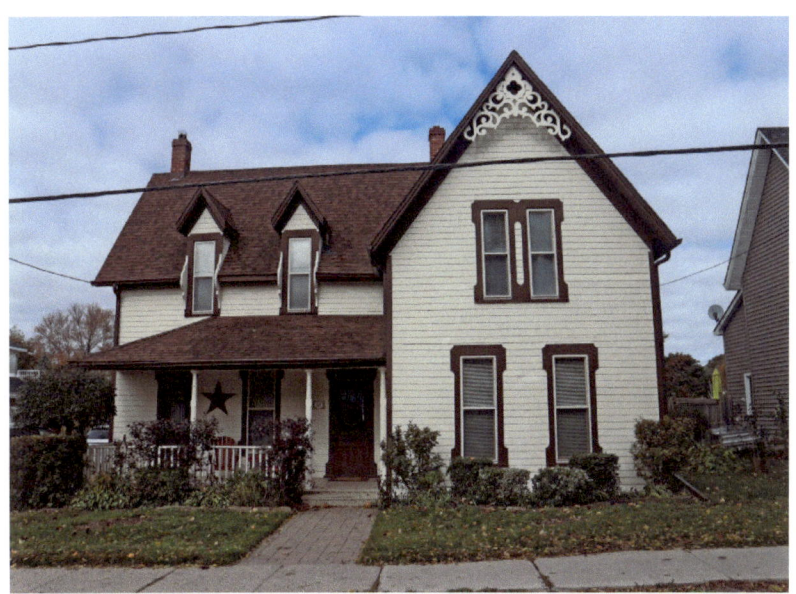

21 Planks Lane – bargeboard trim on gable, dormers

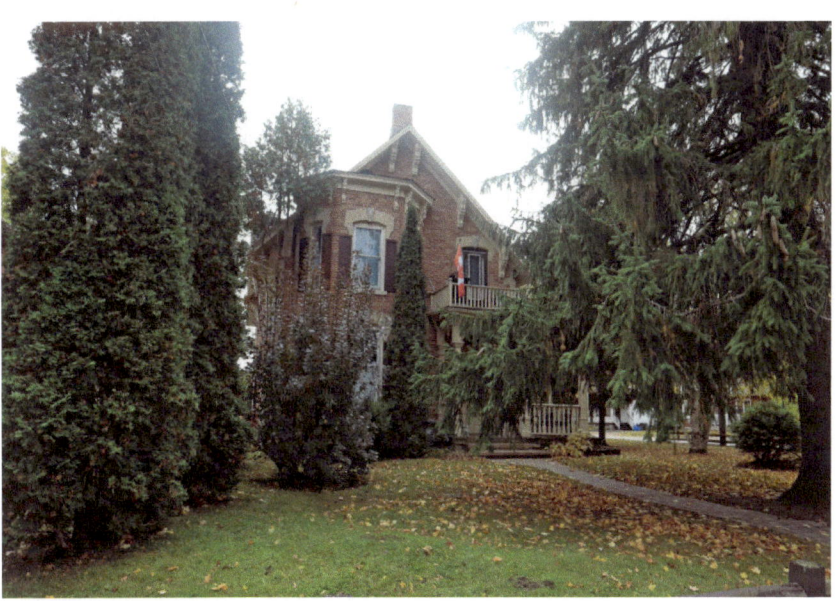

34 Planks Lane - Franklin Davis House – He was a piano teacher and salesman with the Uxbridge Piano and Organ Factory. This house is in late Victorian Style.

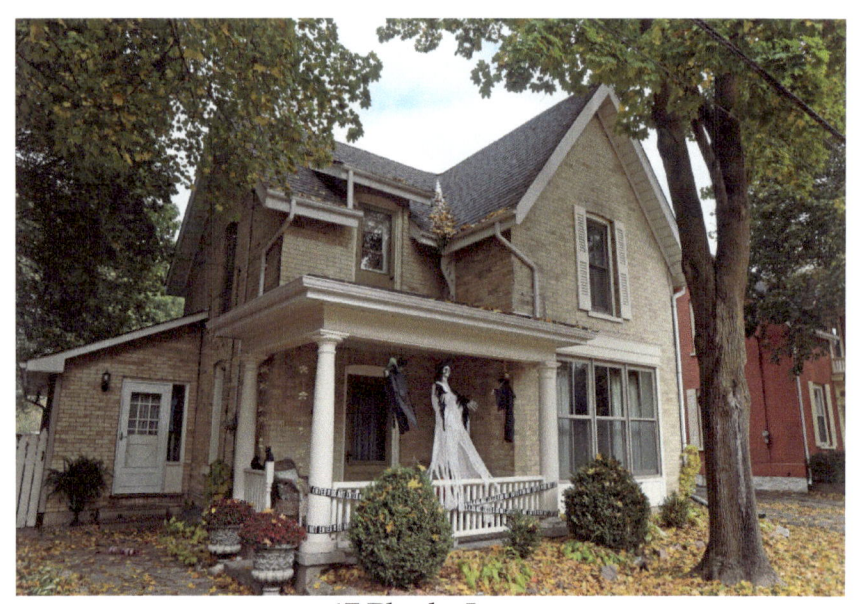

47 Planks Lane

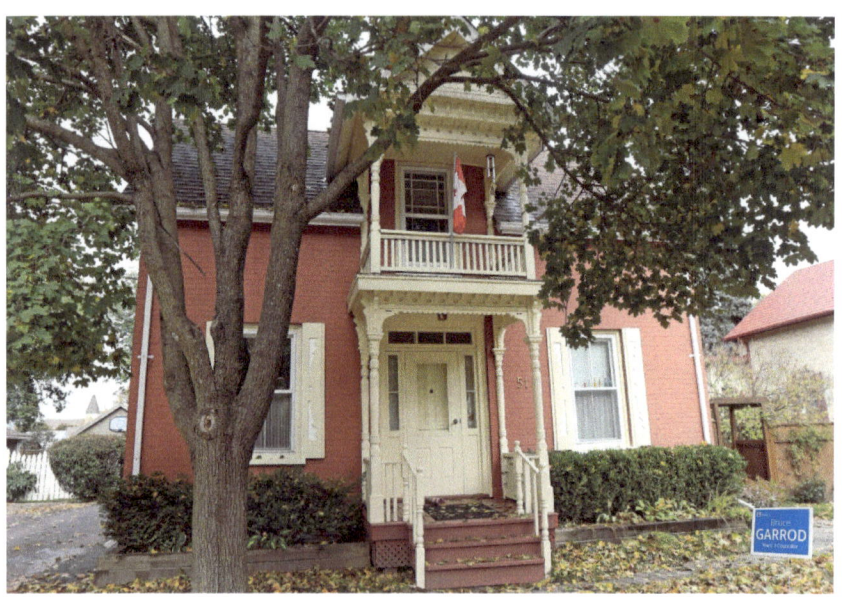

51 Planks Lane

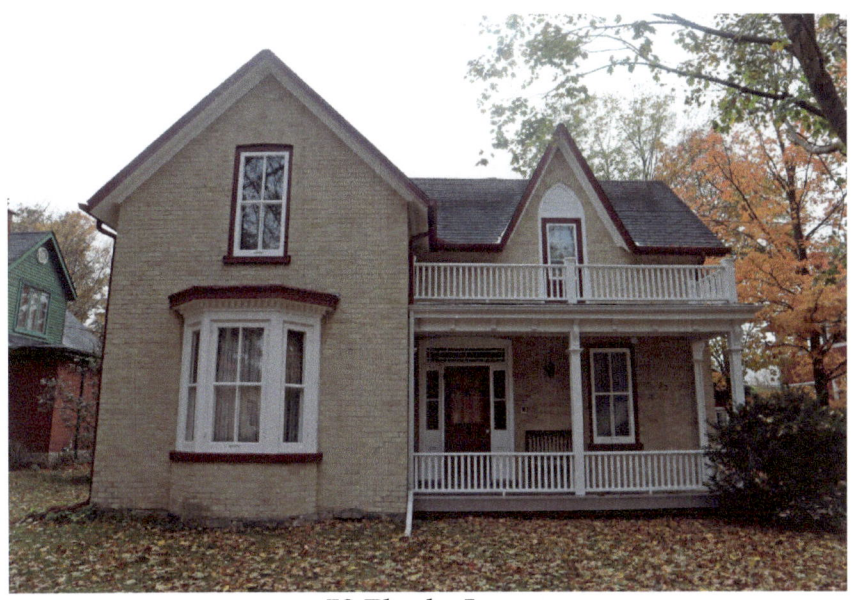

52 Planks Lane

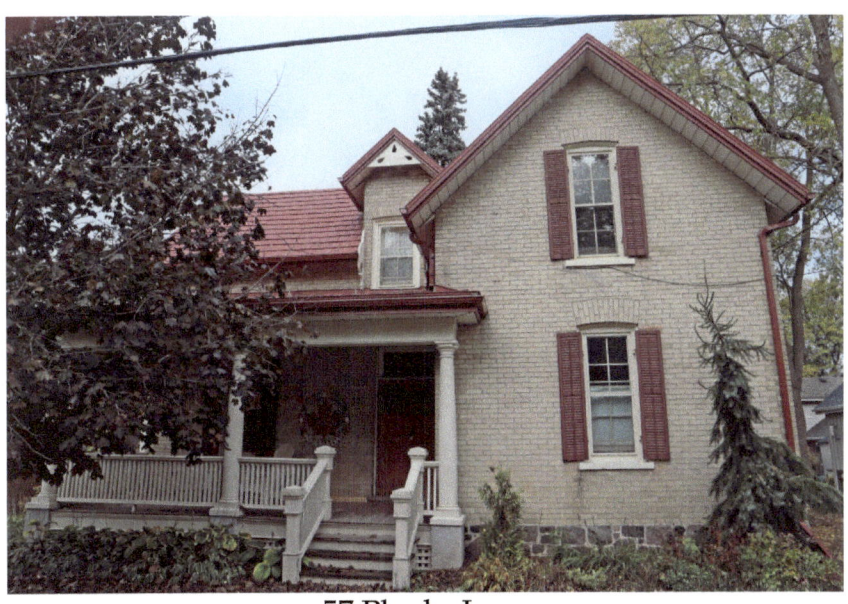

57 Planks Lane

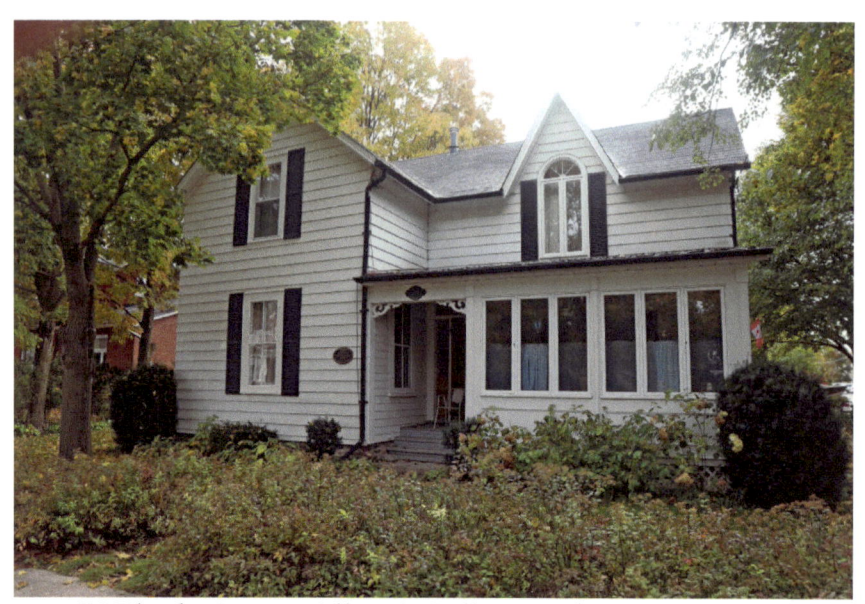

74 Planks Lane - Allan & Polly Wright House, Polly granddaughter of J.P. Plank, (1880-1913) - c. 1879

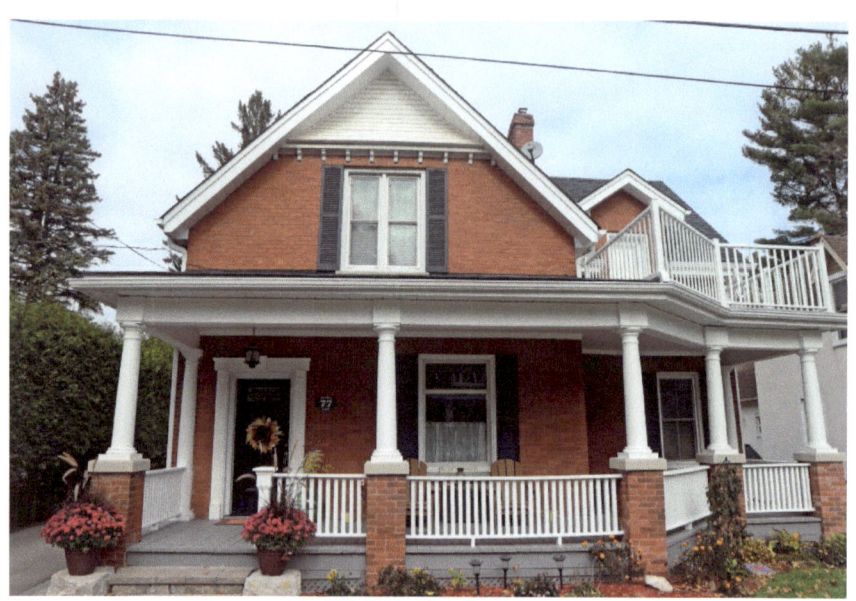

77 Planks Lane

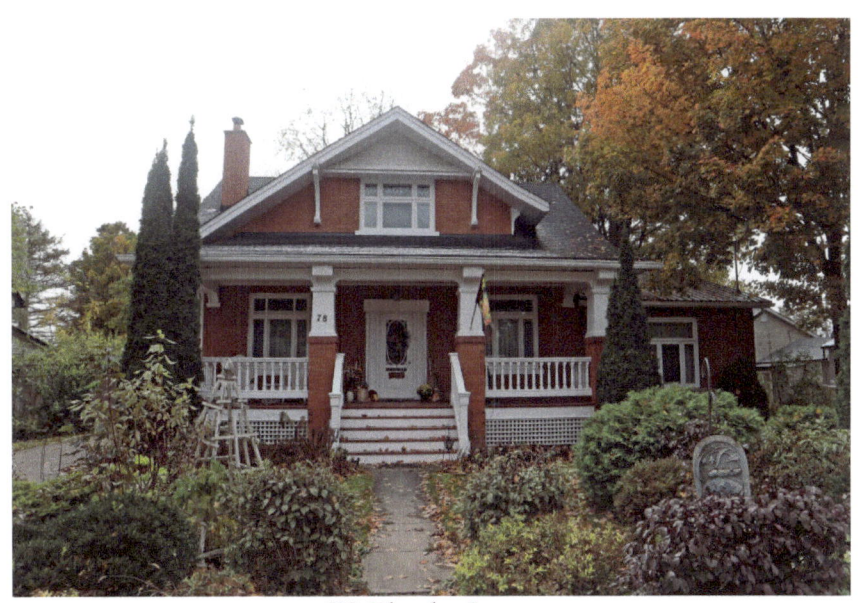

78 Planks Lane

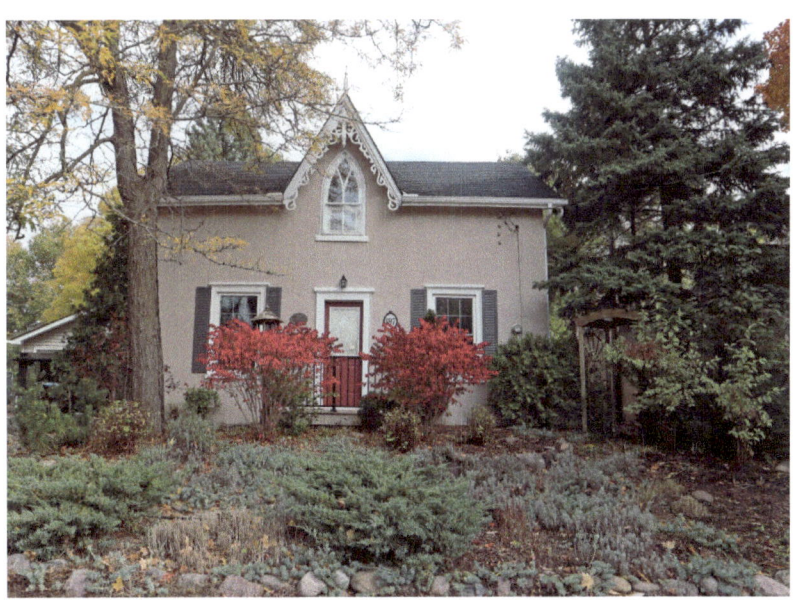

197 East Street - William & Mary Darlington House, Soda Water Manufacturer – c. 1890

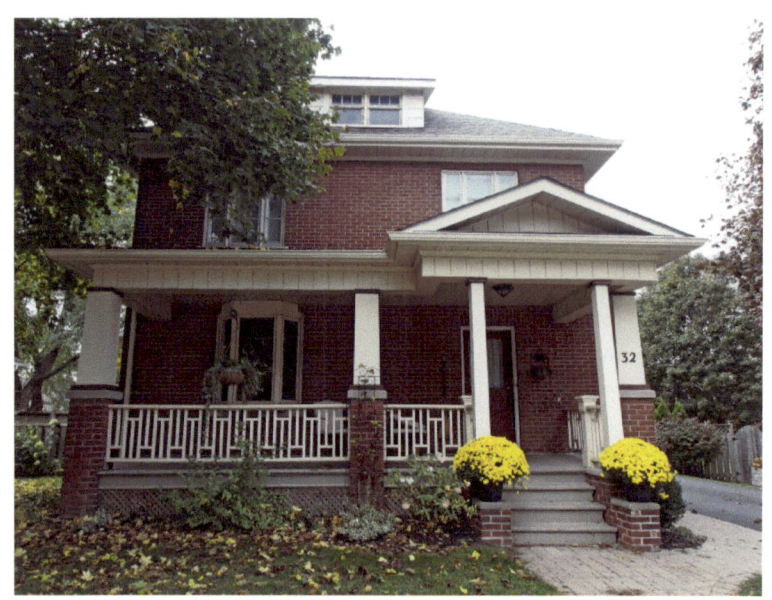

32 Marietta Street

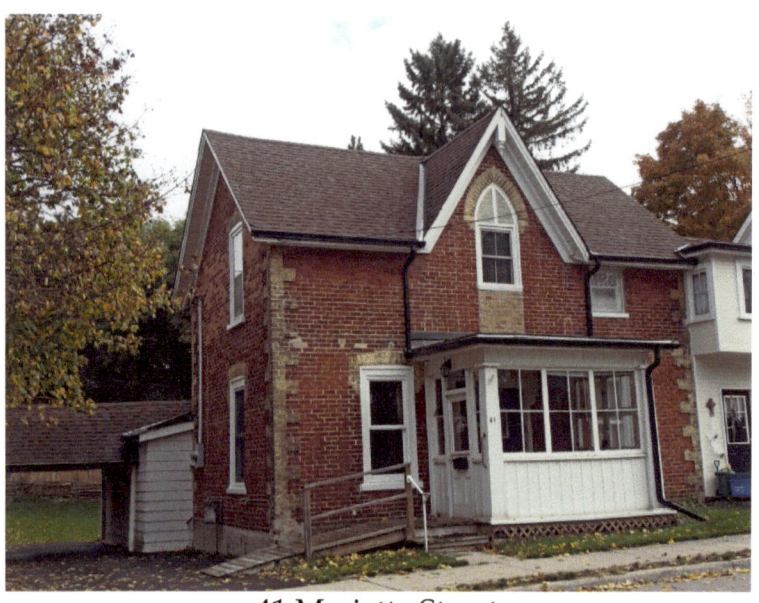

41 Marietta Street

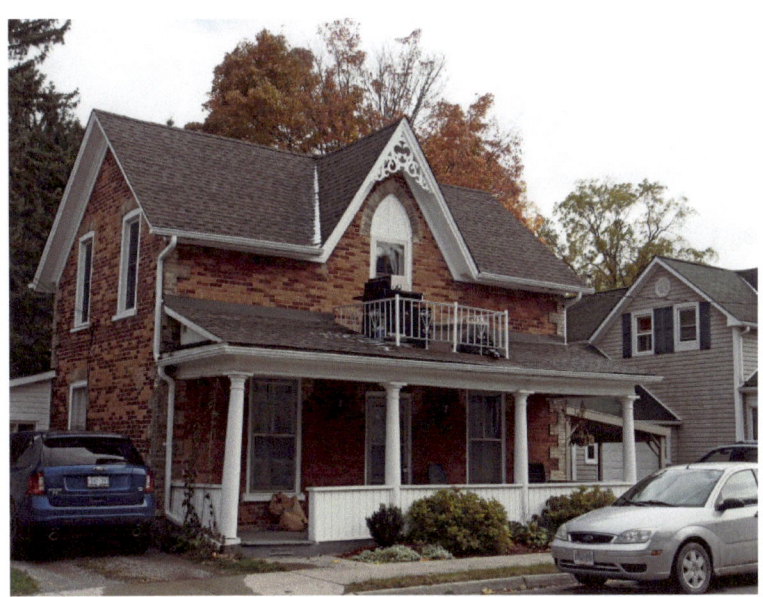

45 Marietta Street

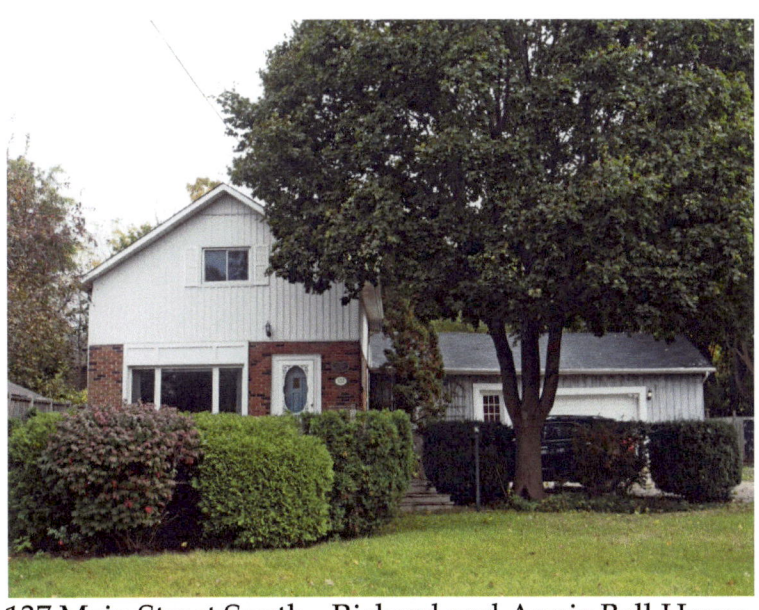

137 Main Street South - Richard and Annie Bell House, Yeoman – c. 1872

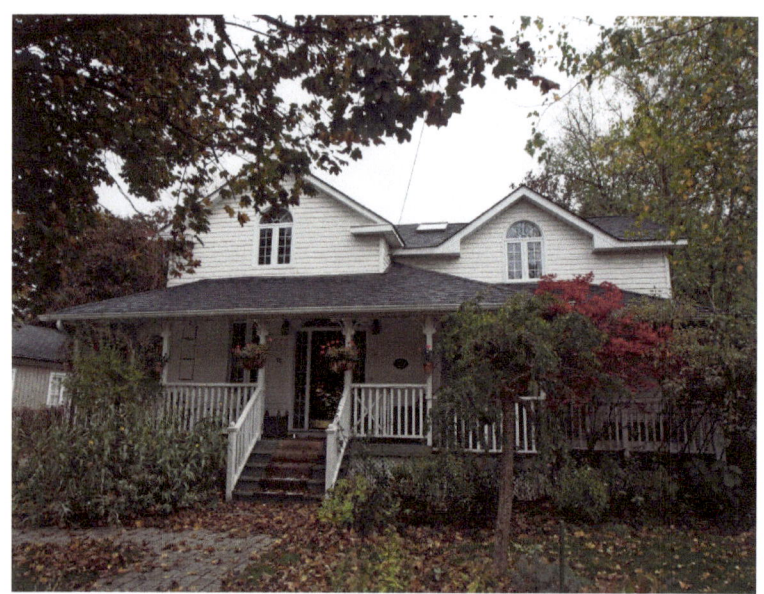

127 Main Street South – Pond House

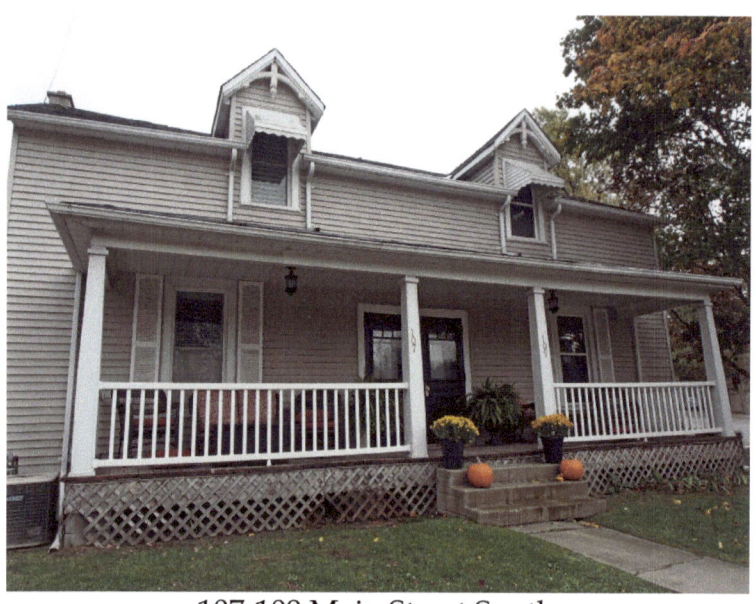

107-109 Main Street South

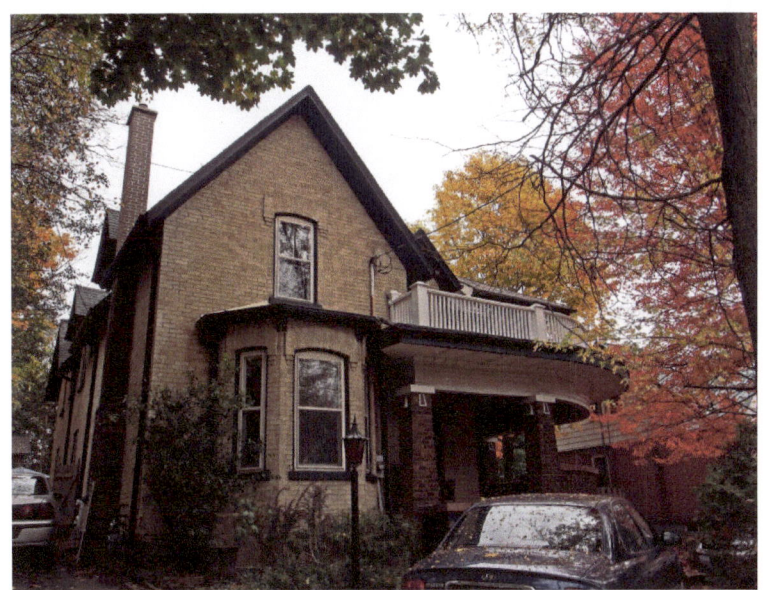

97 Main Street South

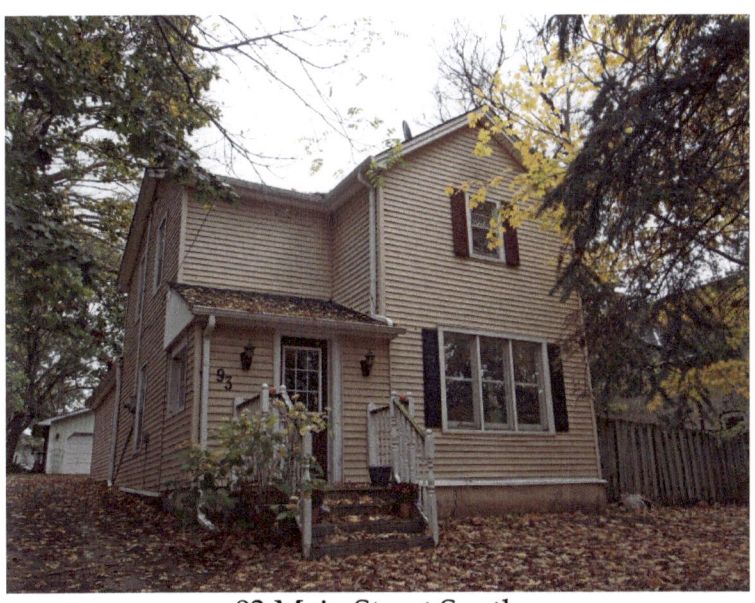

93 Main Street South

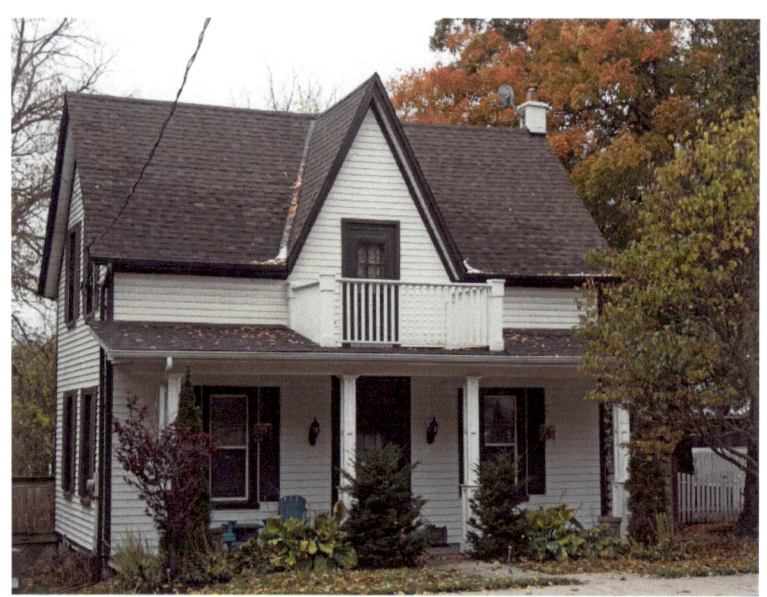

Main Street South

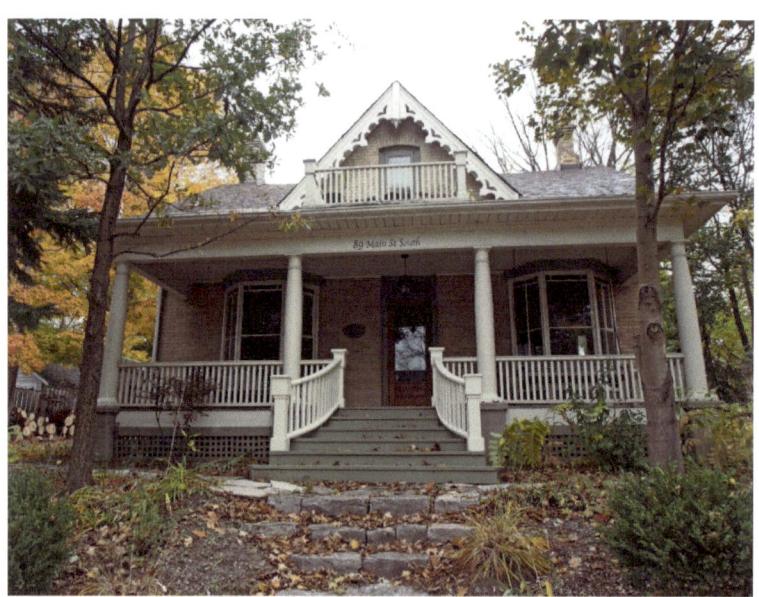

89 Main Street South - William & Amelia Vyvyan House, Tailor (1872-1973) – c. 1869

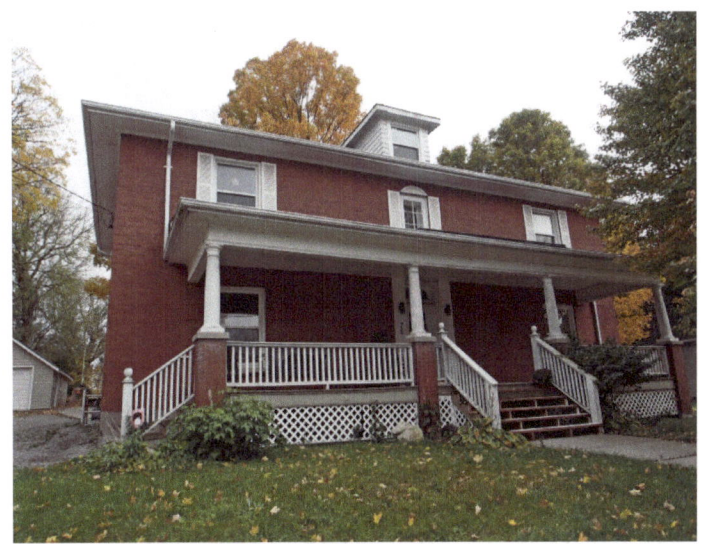

75 Main Street South

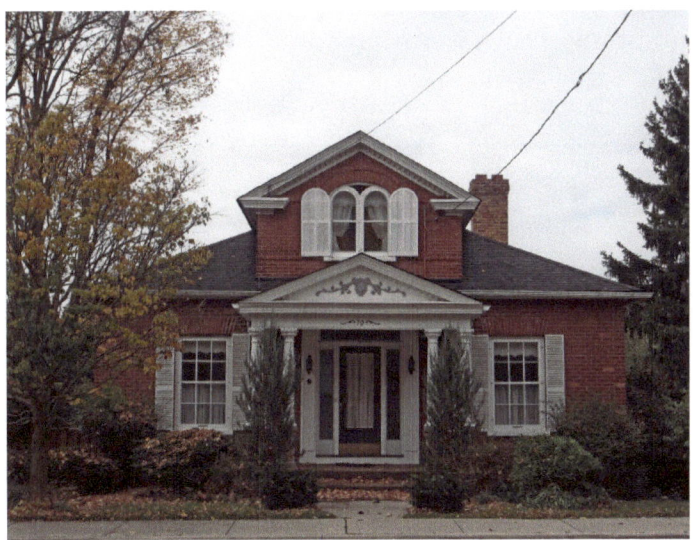

70 Main Street South - Bascom-Williams House - The house was a small square frame house that was later bricked. The property was originally owned by Dr. Joseph Bascom and was transferred to his daughter Mary in 1872. Mary married Alonzo D. Williams who was the first clerk for the Village of Uxbridge and held that position for 27 years.

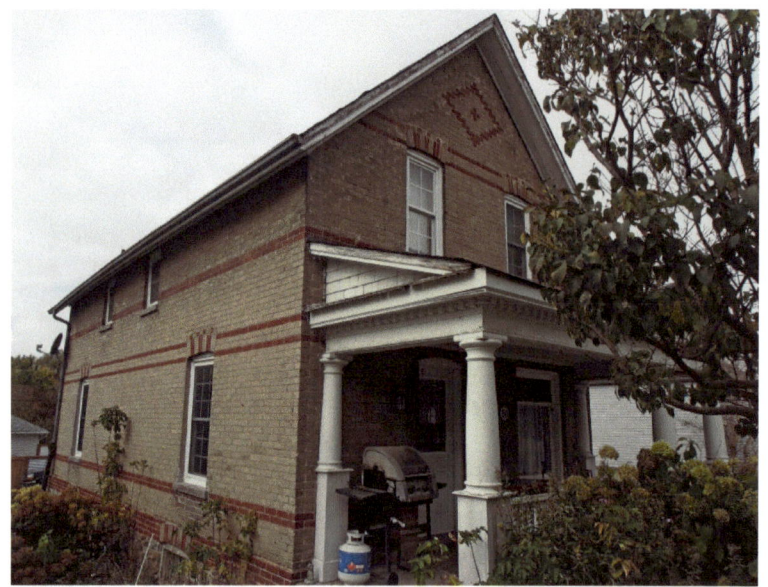
60 Main Street South – banding and dichromatic brickwork

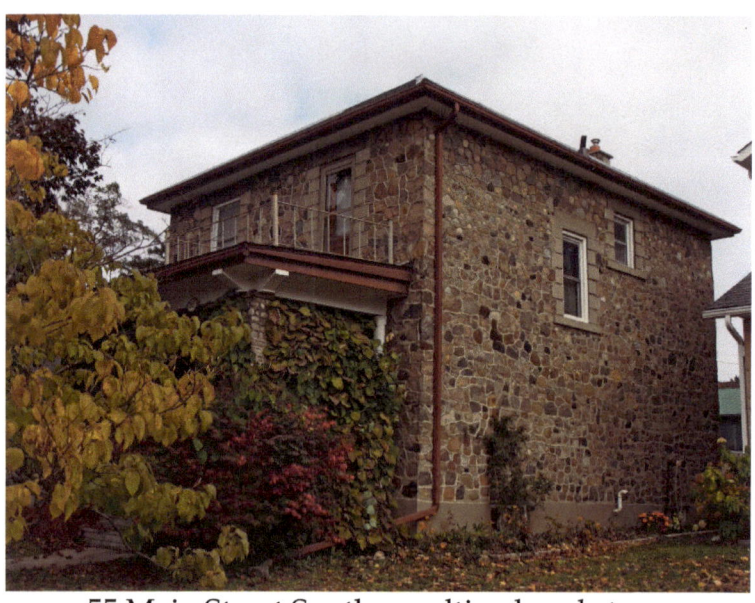
55 Main Street South – multi-colored stone

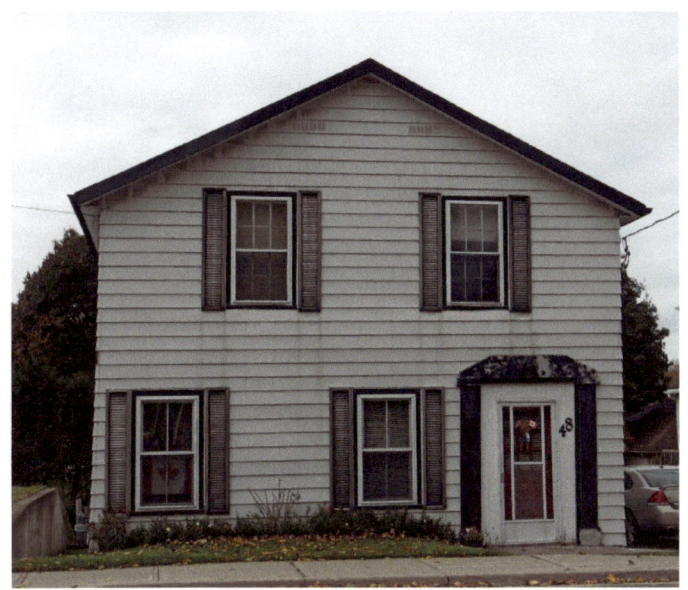

48 Main Street South

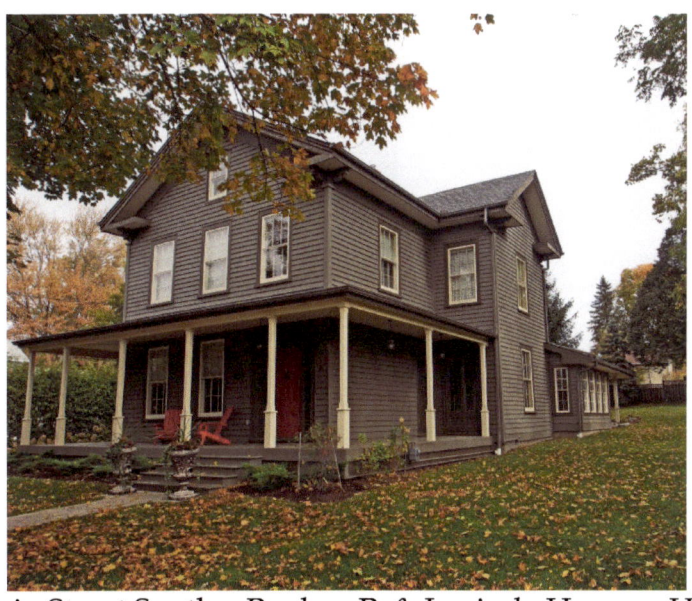

41 Main Street South – Reuben P. & Lucinda Harman House, Reeve of Uxbridge – c. 1868

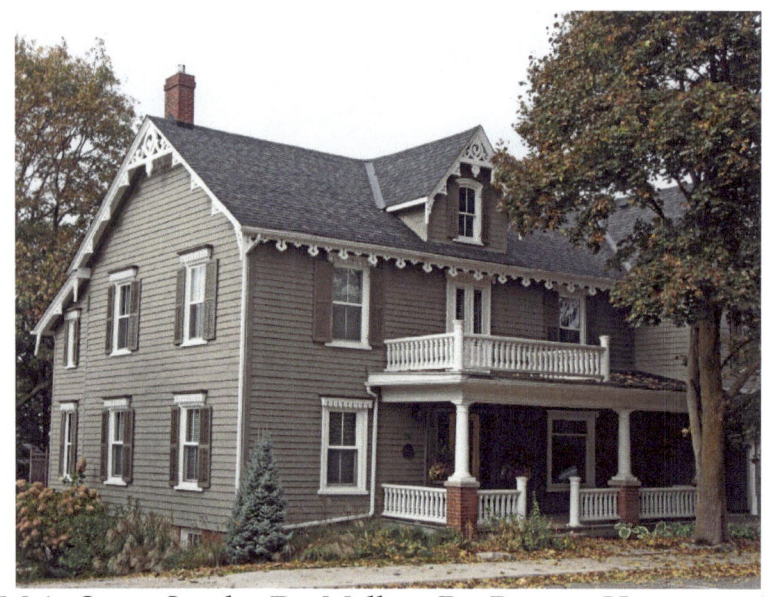

38 Main Street South - Dr. Mellow-Dr. Bascom House – c. 1863

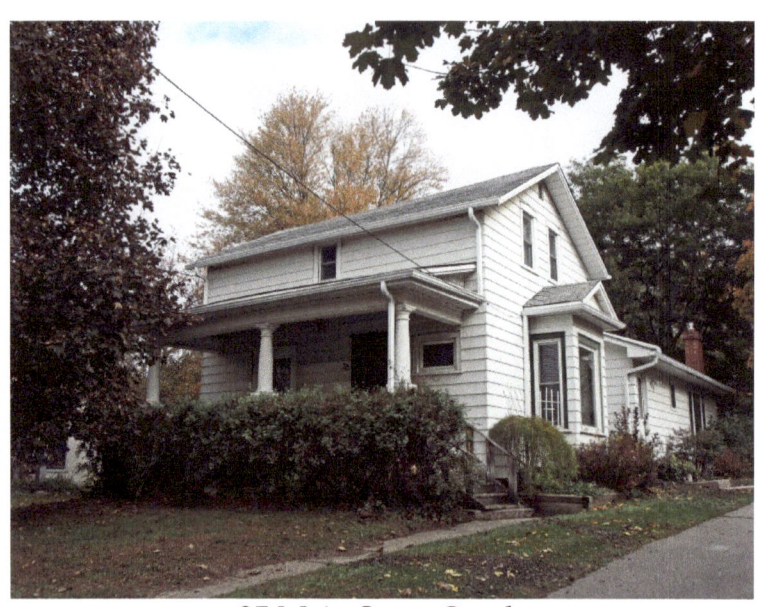

35 Main Street South

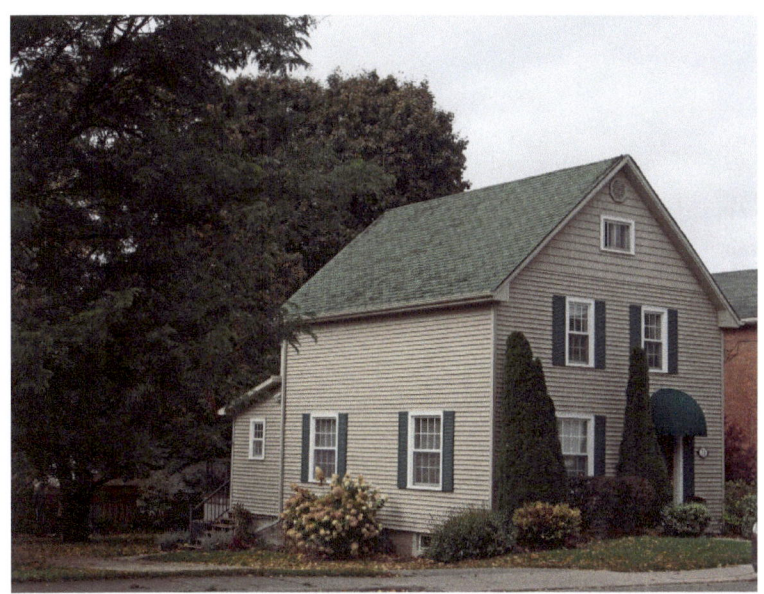

26 Main Street South

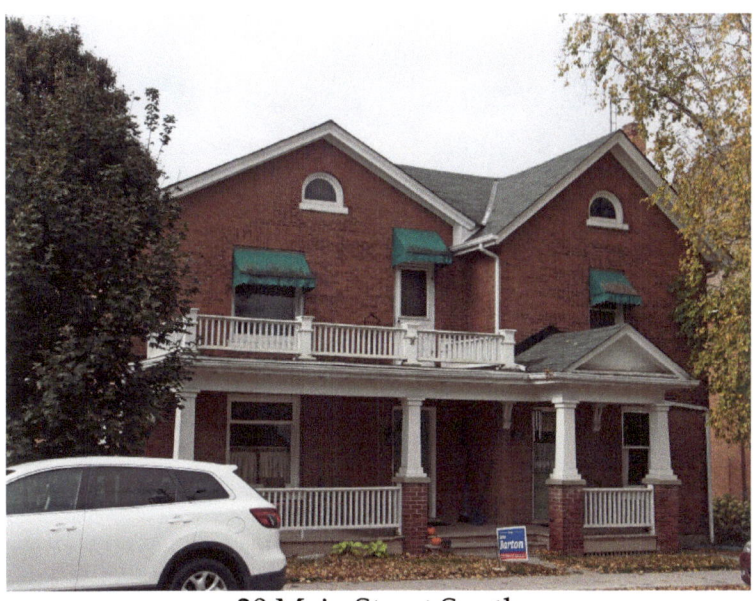

20 Main Street South

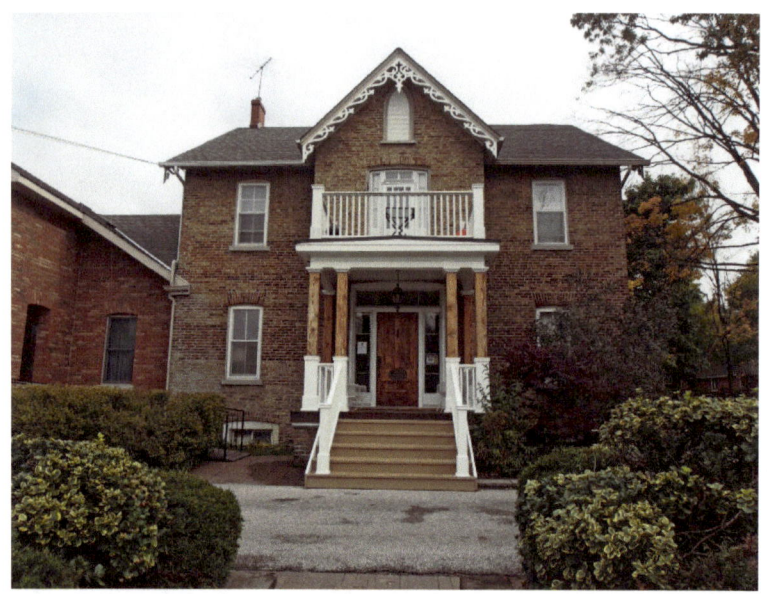

23 Main Street South - c. 1873 - Early Town Founder, John P. Plank bought 100 acres at the corner of Main and Brock Street in 1825. In 1828 he built the first store in Town and the first saw mill at Elgin Pond.

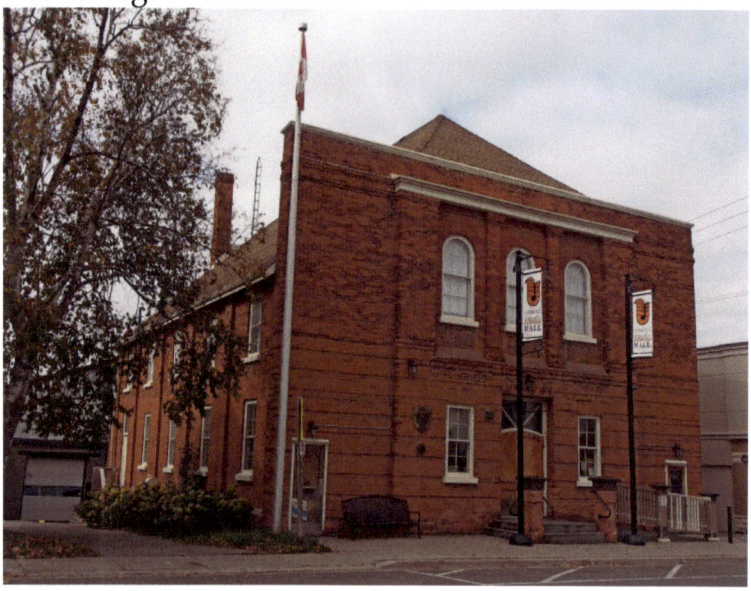

16 Main Street South – 1901 Music Hall

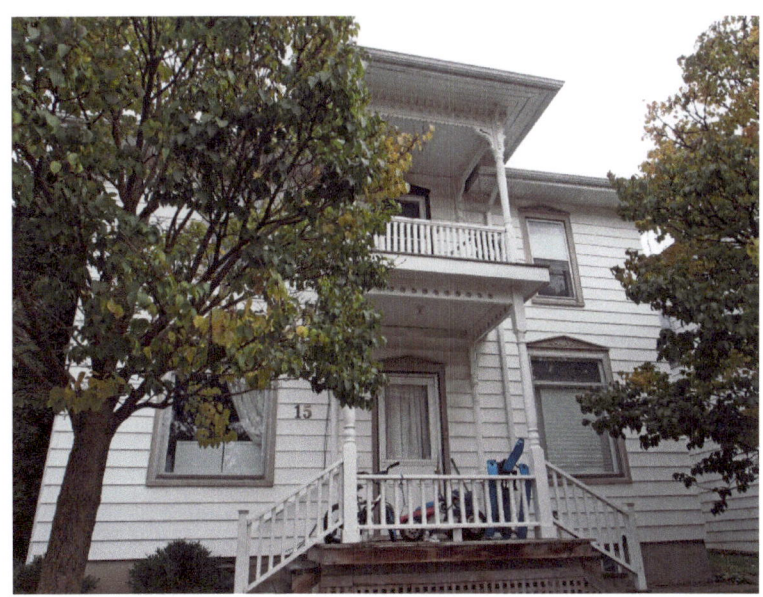
15 Main Street South

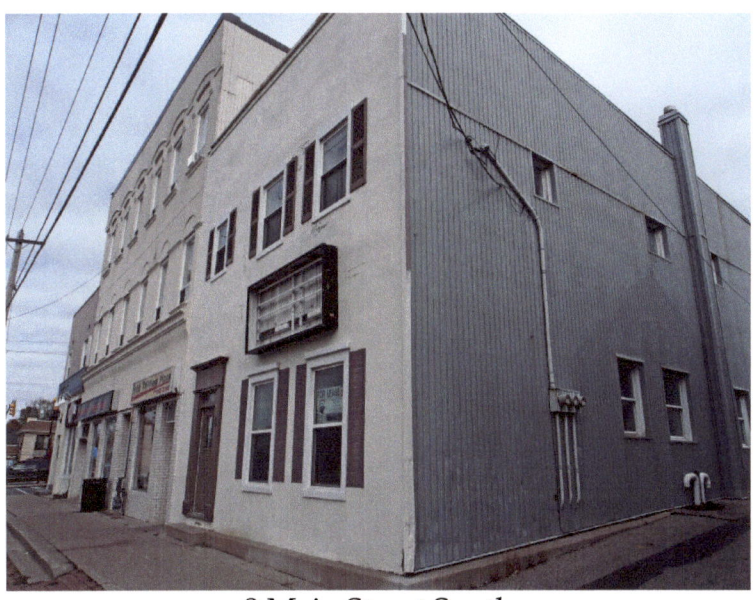
9 Main Street South

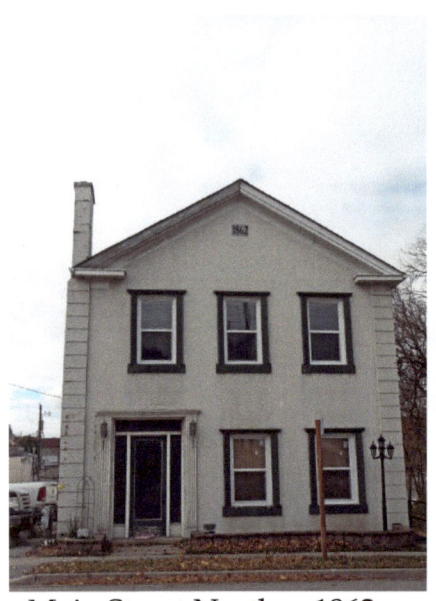
Main Street North c. 1862
Cornice return on gable

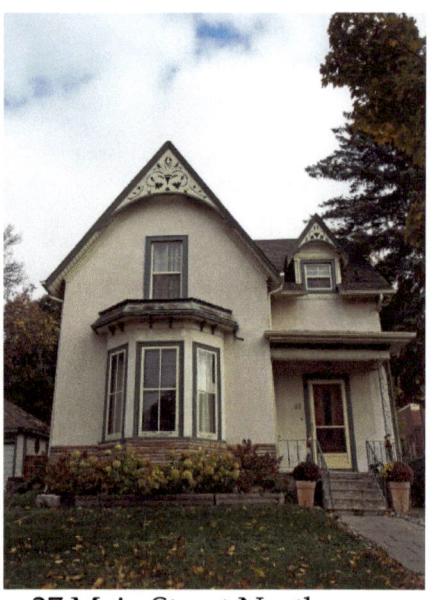
27 Main Street North
verge board trim on gables,
bay window with brackets

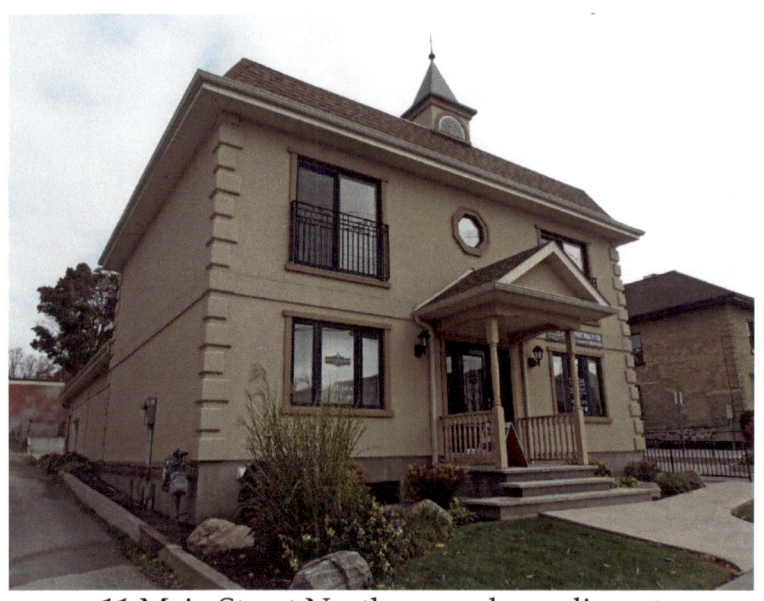
11 Main Street North – cupola, pediment

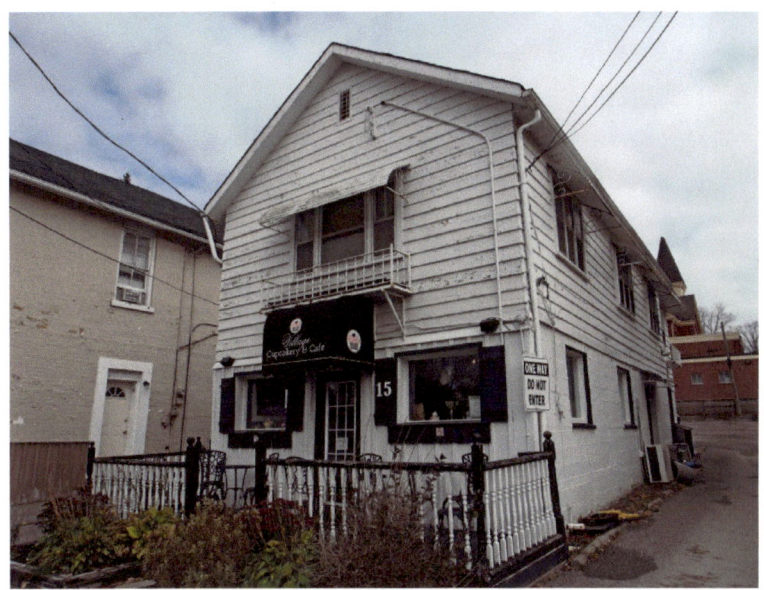

15 Main Street North – Village Cupcakery & Cafe

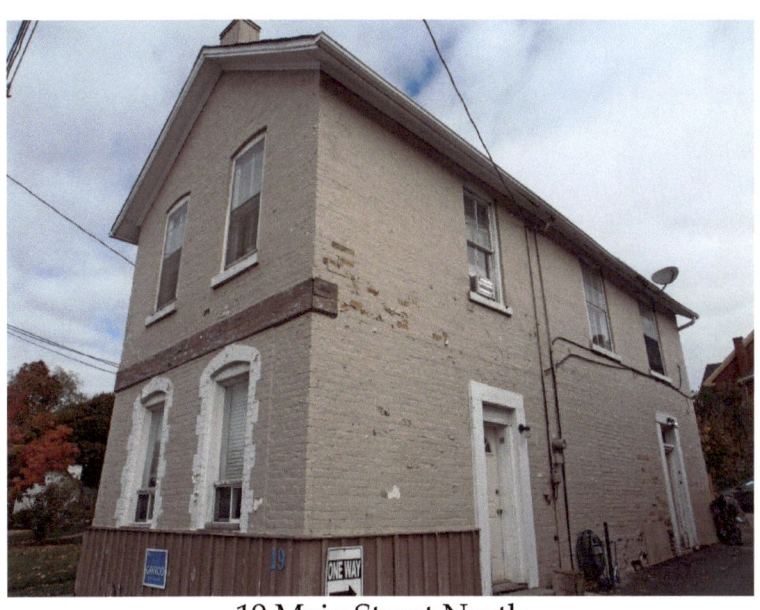

19 Main Street North

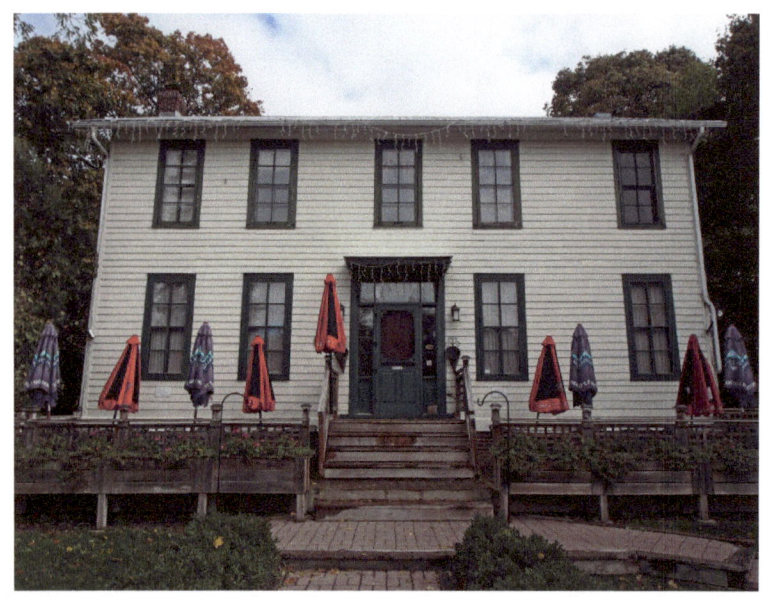

39 Main Street North – Former Commercial Hotel Building and Property - Hobby Horse Arms – c. 1868 – Georgian style

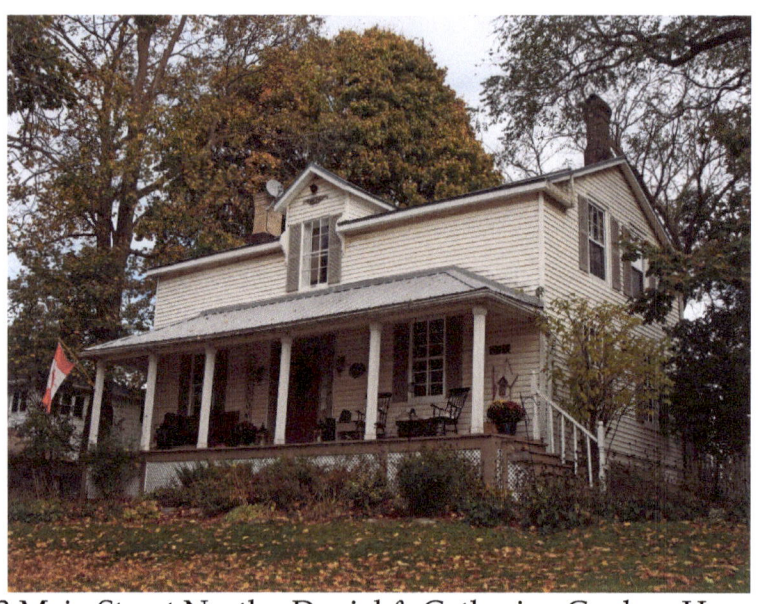

43 Main Street North - Daniel & Catherine Conboy House, Carriage & Sleigh Builder – c. 1874

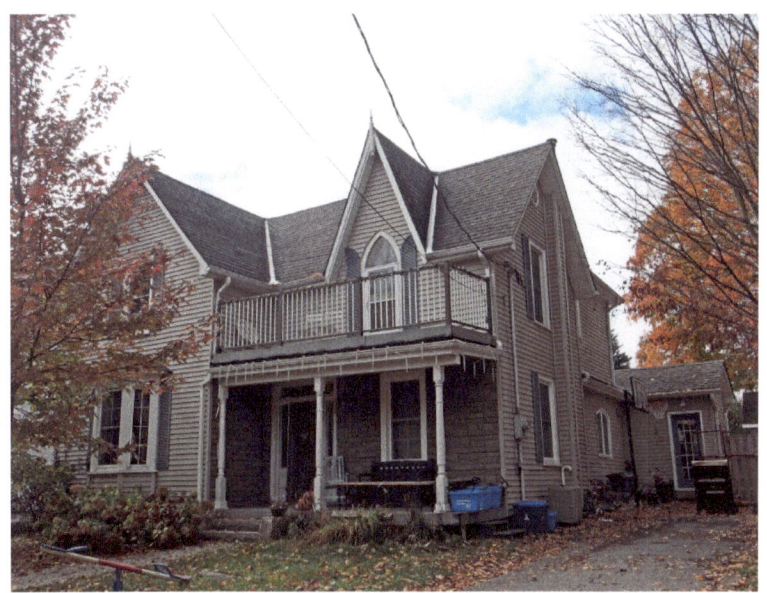

Franklin Street

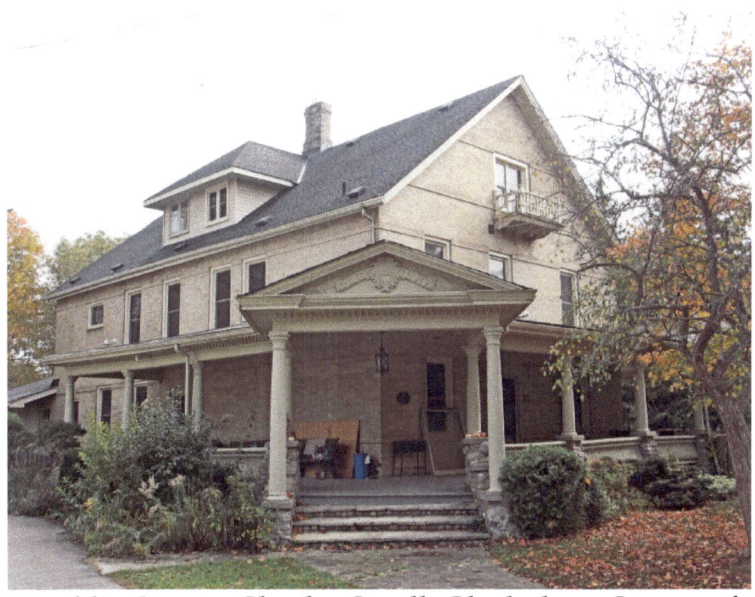

23 Franklin Street - Charles Small, Gleeholme, Owner of the Uxbridge Piano & Organ Company – c. 1901

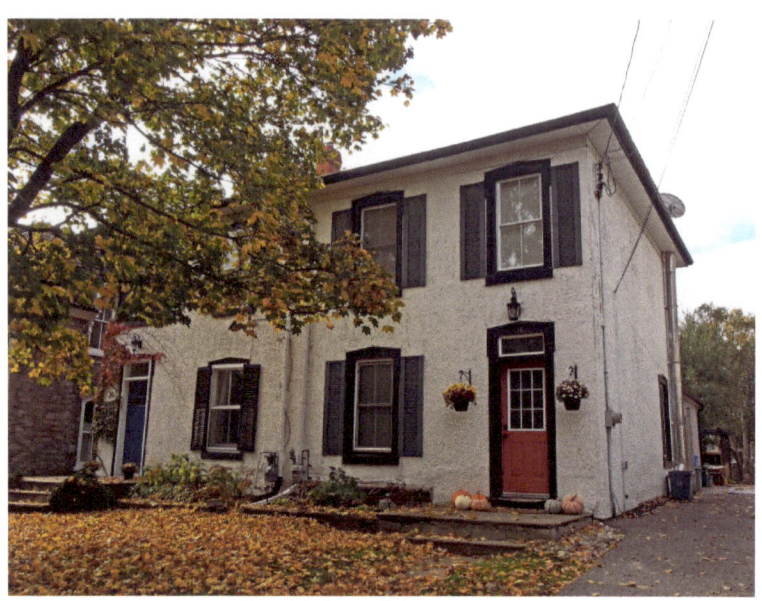

24-26 Franklin Street

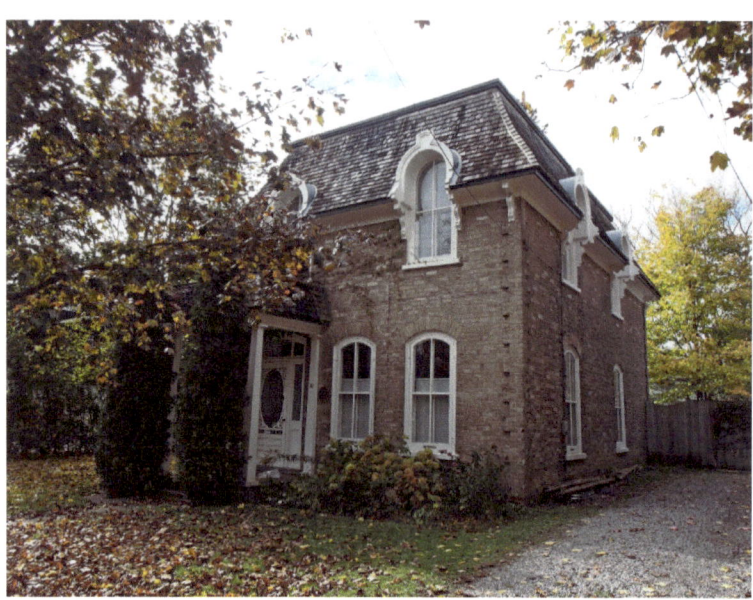

30 Franklin Street - Halbert Hardy House – A. S. Hardy, tuner – c. 1875 - mansard-type roof, window hoods

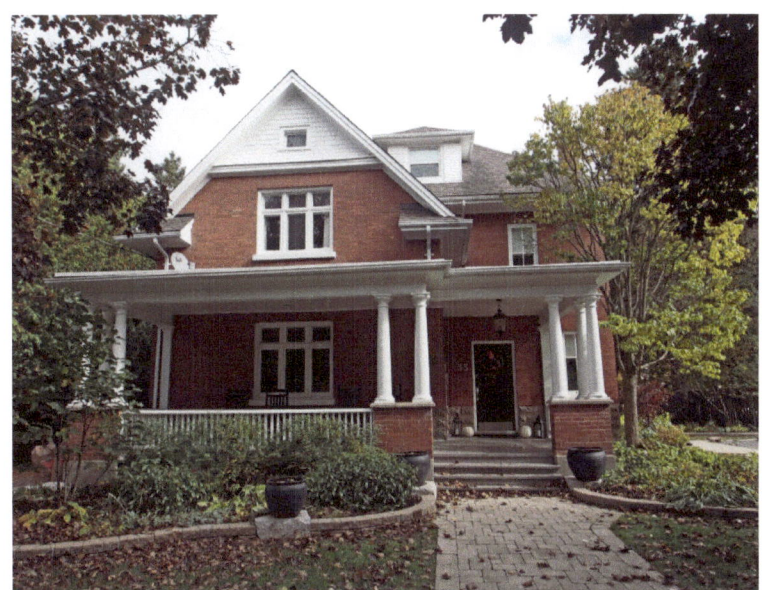

33 Franklin Street - William & Abigail Hamilton House, Postmaster/Mayor/Magistrate – c. 1881

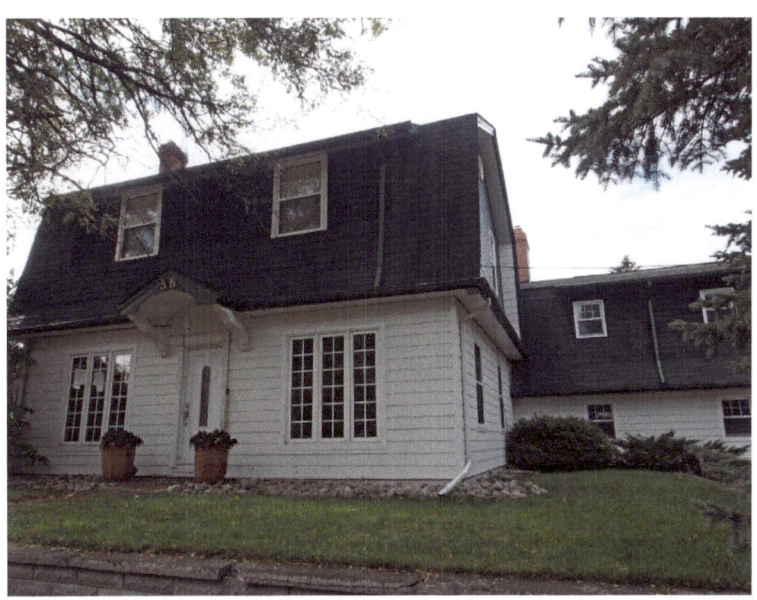

36 Franklin Street – Neo-Colonial – gambrel roof

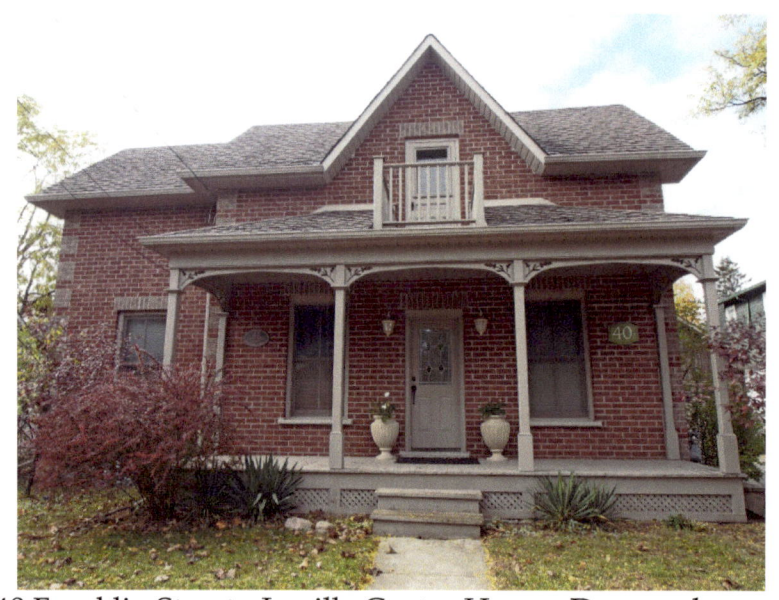

40 Franklin Street - Lucille Coates House, Dressmaker – c. 1876

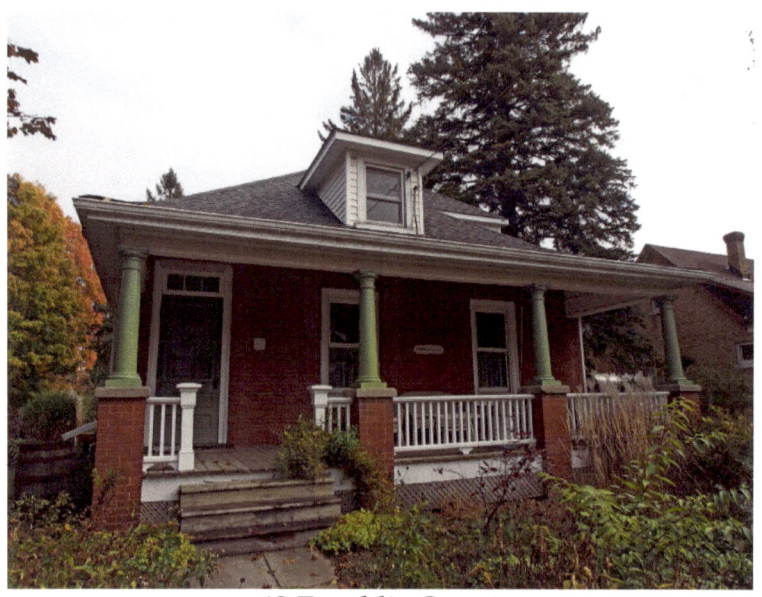

43 Franklin Street

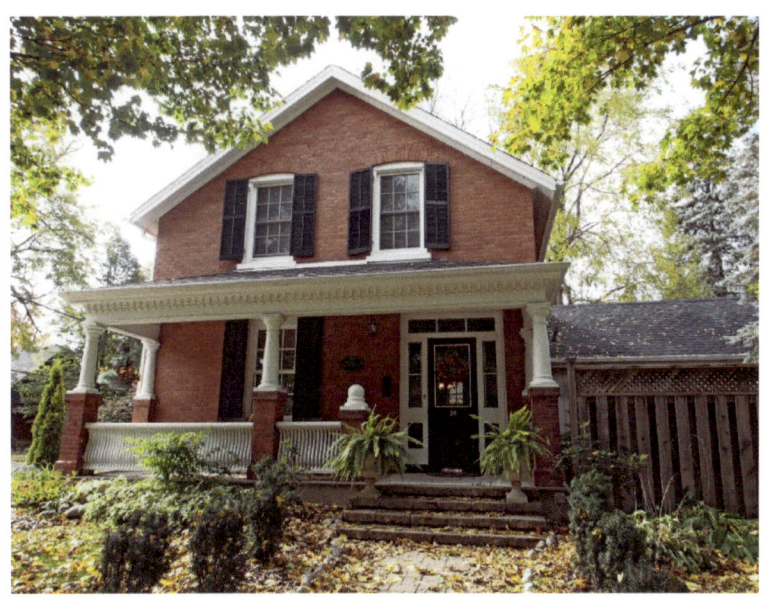

50 Franklin Street - Benjamin Kester Jones House, Carpenter & Cabinetmaker – c. 1872

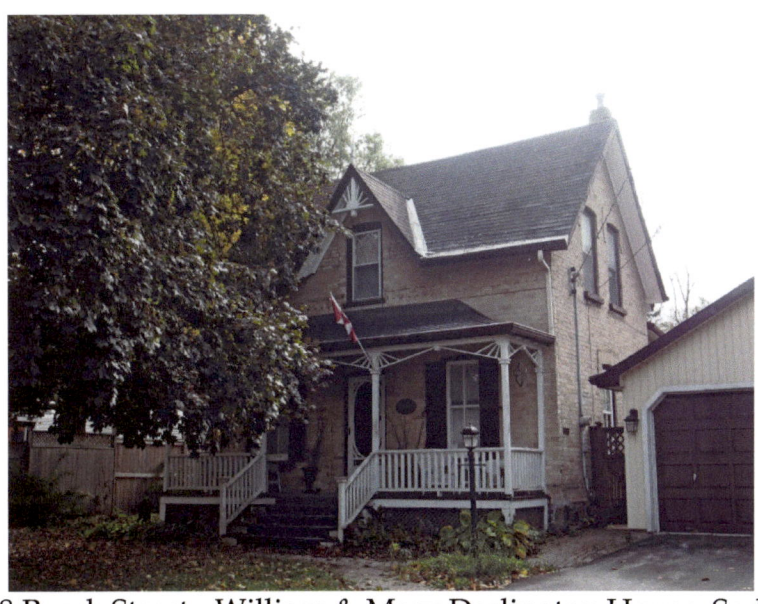

68 Reach Street - William & Mary Darlington House, Soda Water Manufacturer – c. 1871

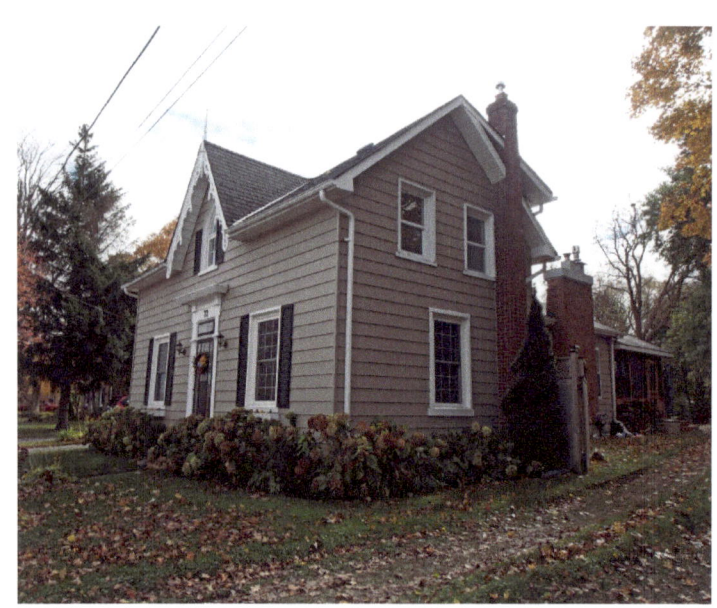

72 Reach Street

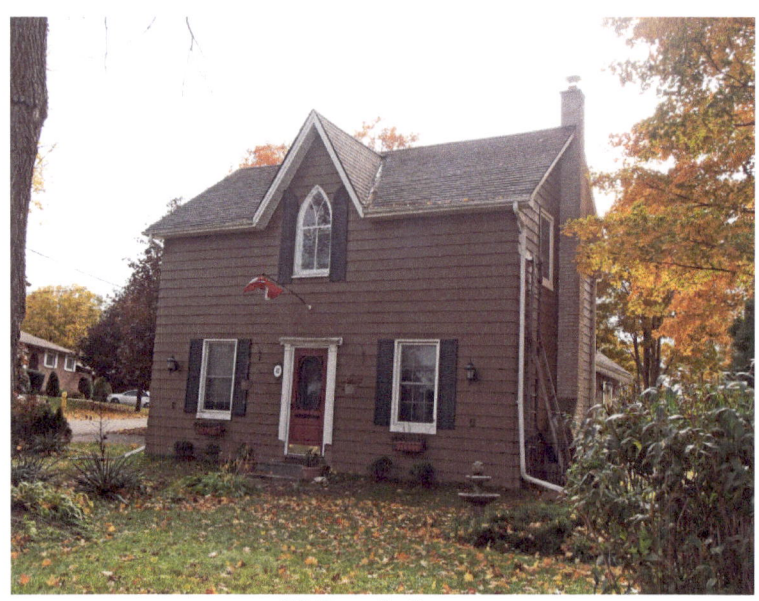

82 Reach Street

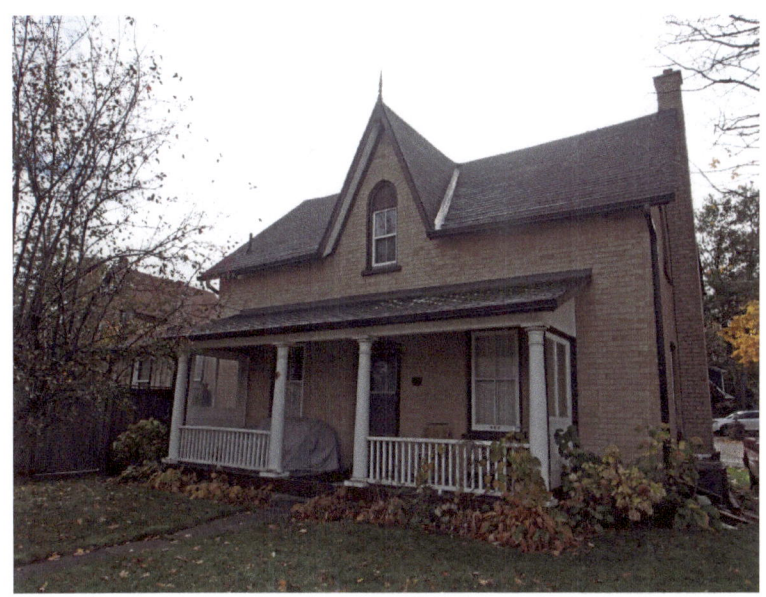

90 Reach Street

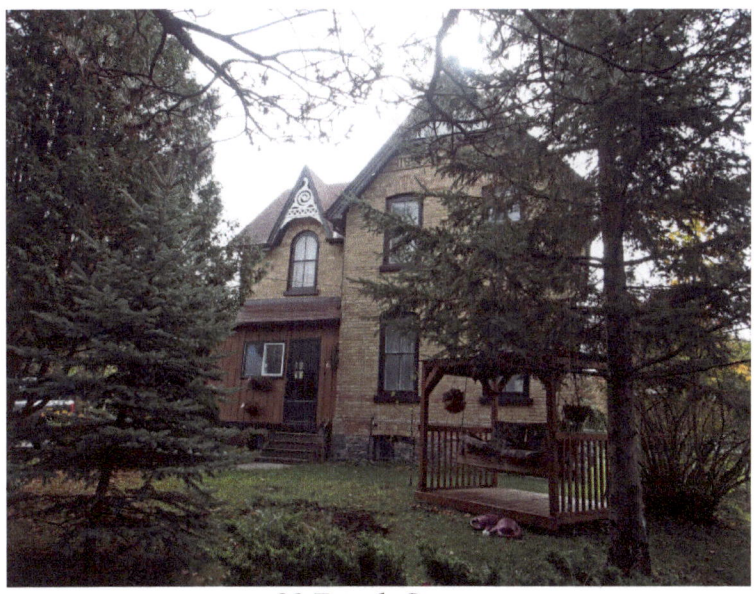

98 Reach Street

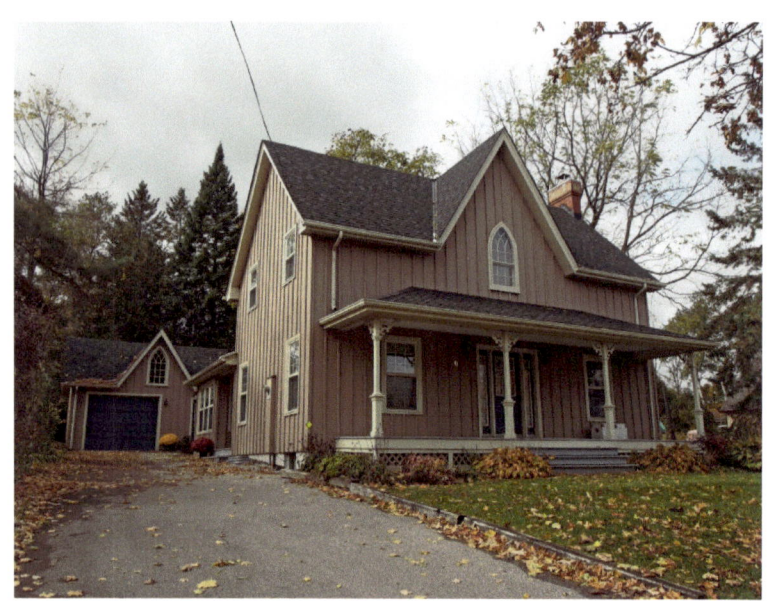

16 Cedar Street North

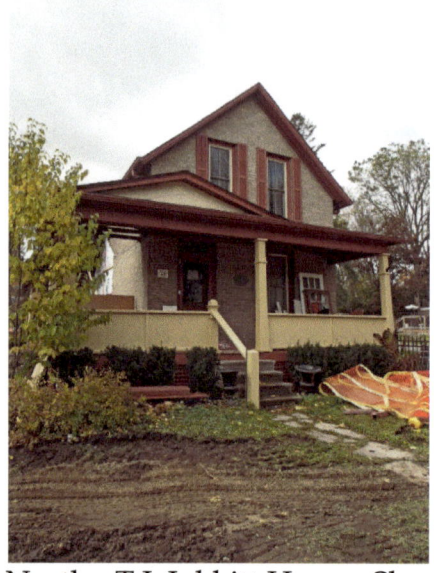

24 Cedar Street North - T.J. Jobbitt House, Shoemaker – c. 1875

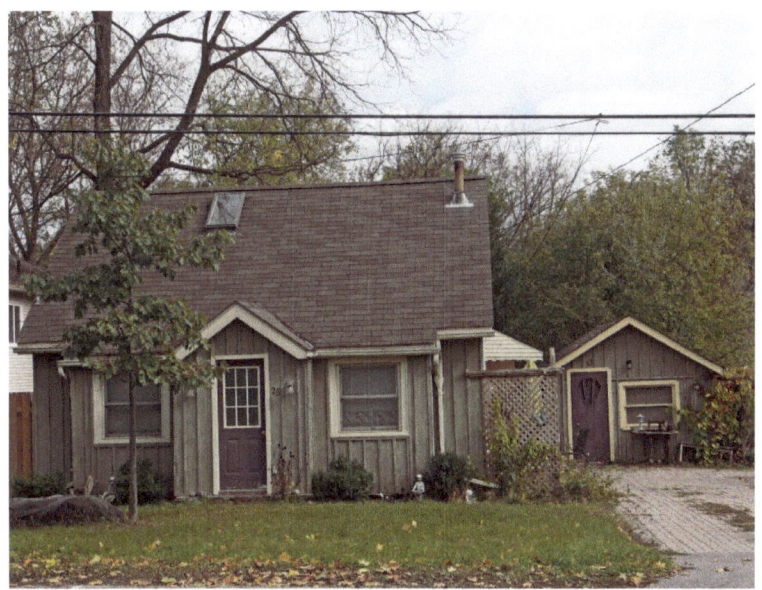

25 Cedar Street North

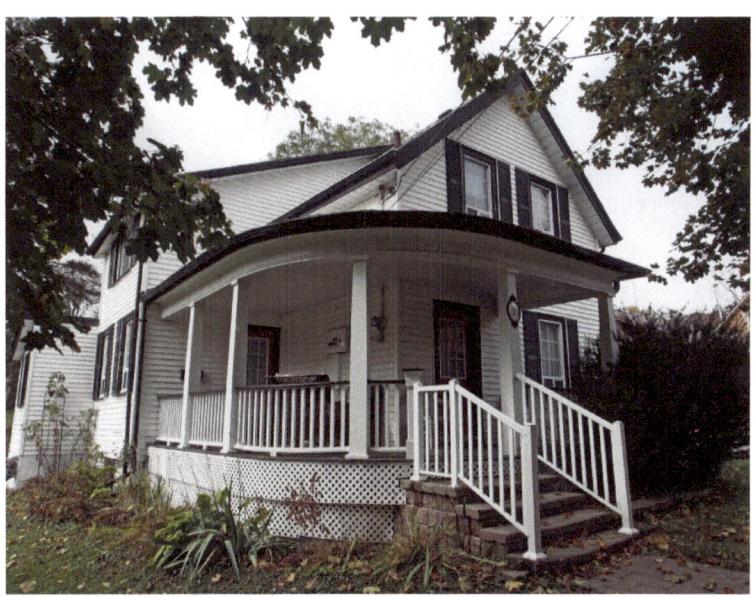

30 Cedar Street North

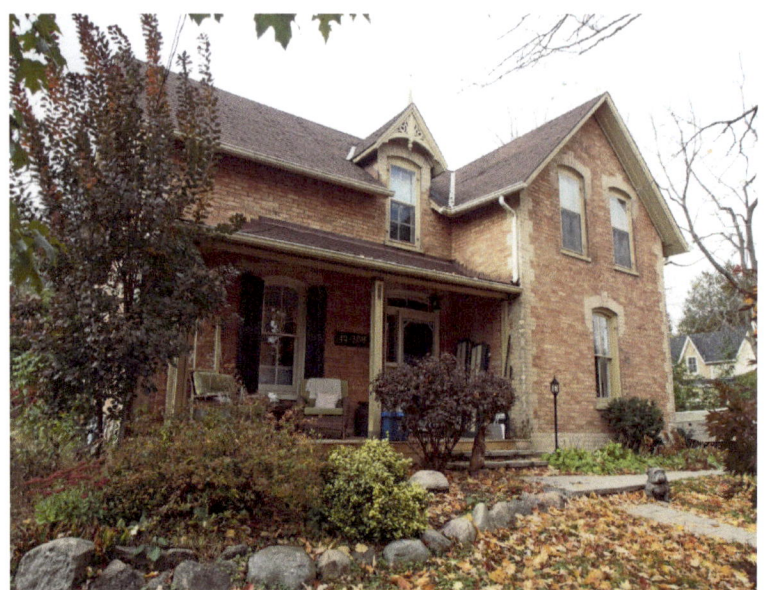

42 Cedar Street North

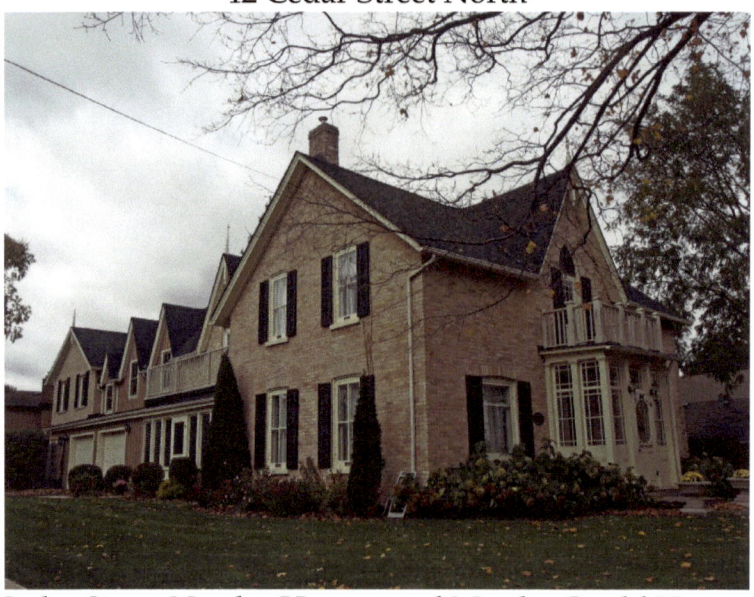

54 Cedar Street North - Harvey and Martha Gould House – c. 1877 - T-shaped 1½ storey white brick house built by Joseph Gould (merchant and miller). In 1886 it was purchased by Harvey Gould a former Mayor of Uxbridge, County Warden.

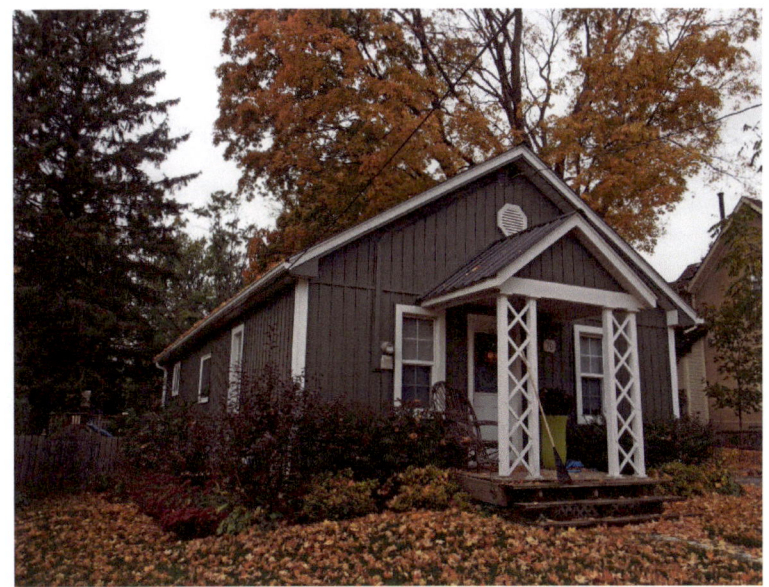

70 Cedar Street North

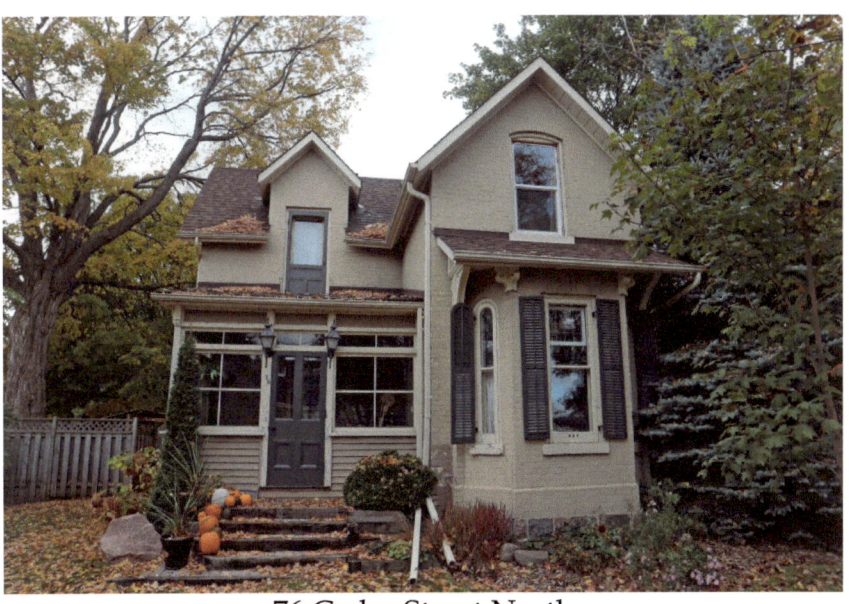

76 Cedar Street North

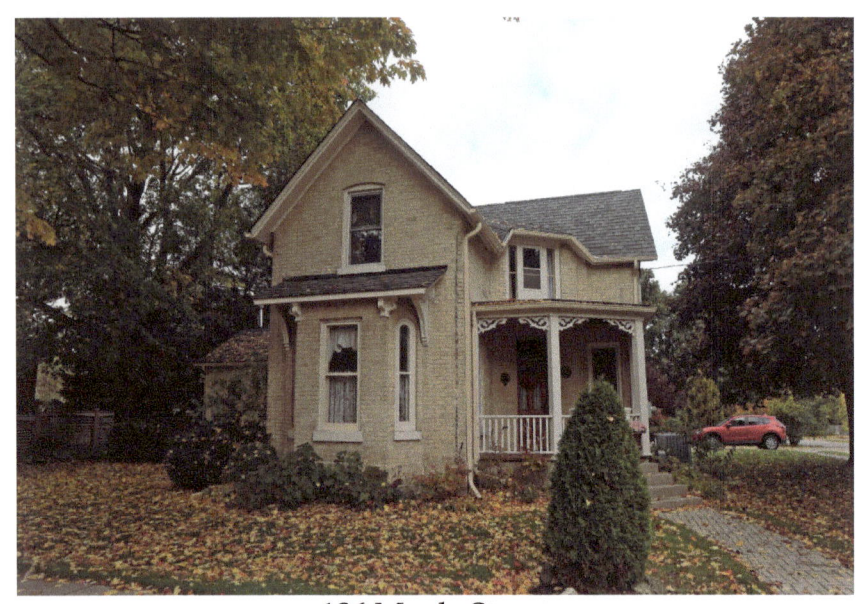

186 Maple Street

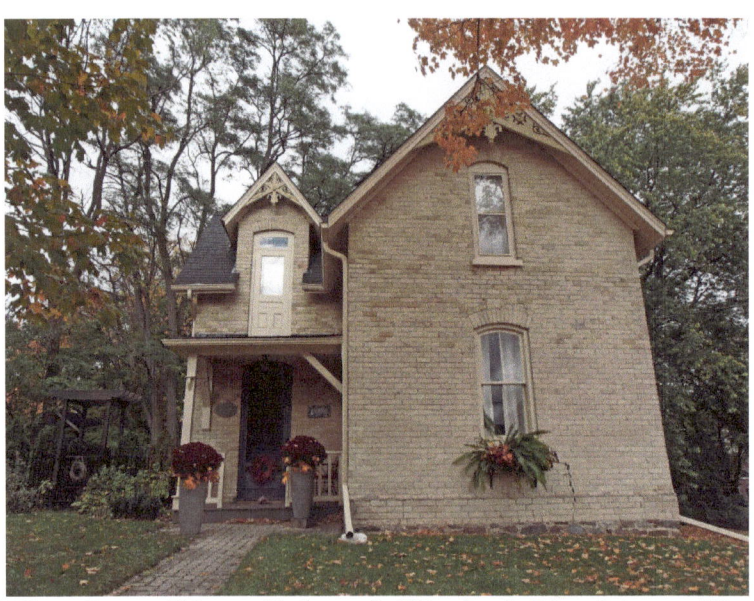

169 King Street West - Robert & Elizabeth Hutchinson House, Farmer & Builder (1906-1911) – c. 1886

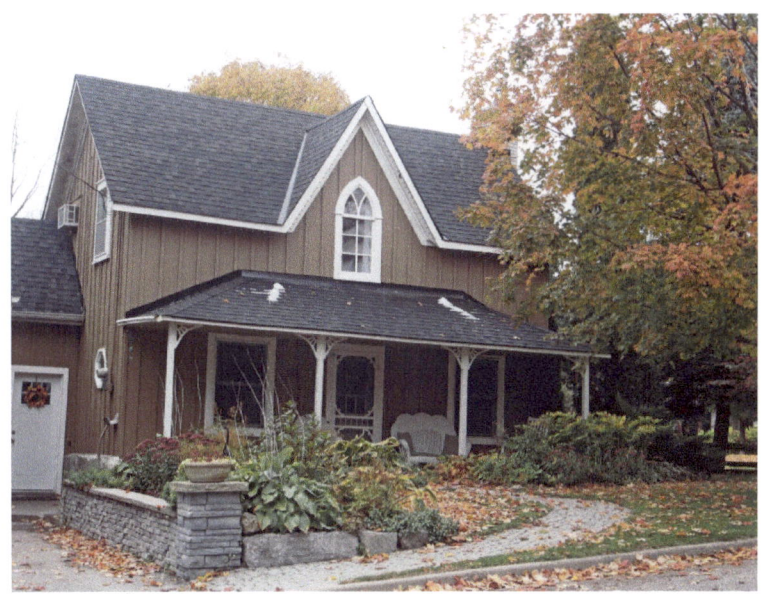

174 King Street West

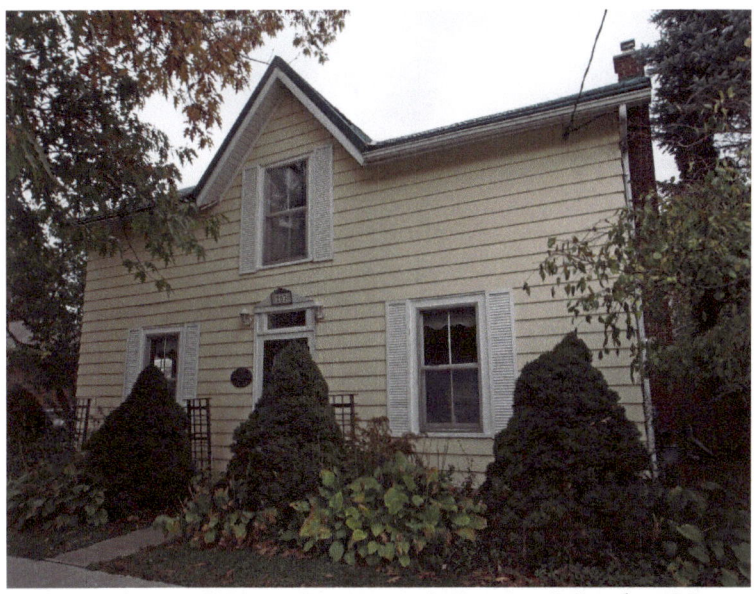

203 King Street West - Lorenzo & Louisa Morden House, Painter (1890-1902) – c. 1890

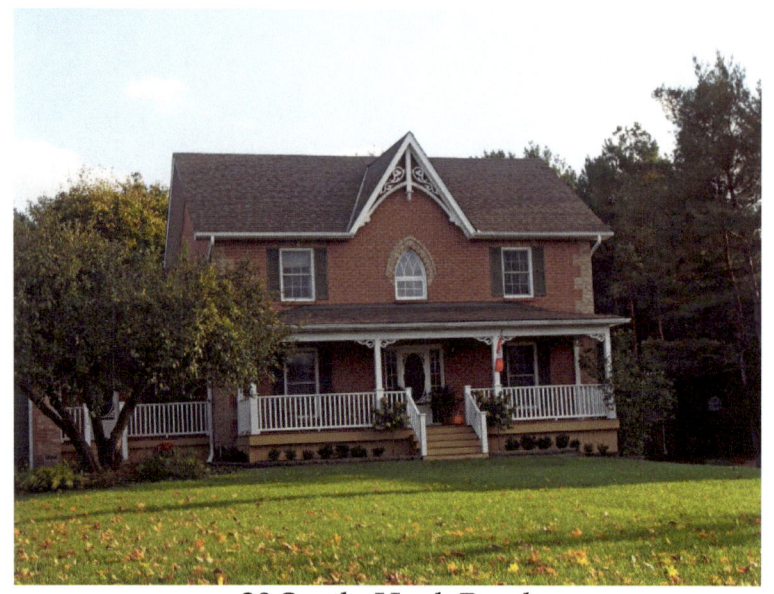

20 Sandy Hook Road

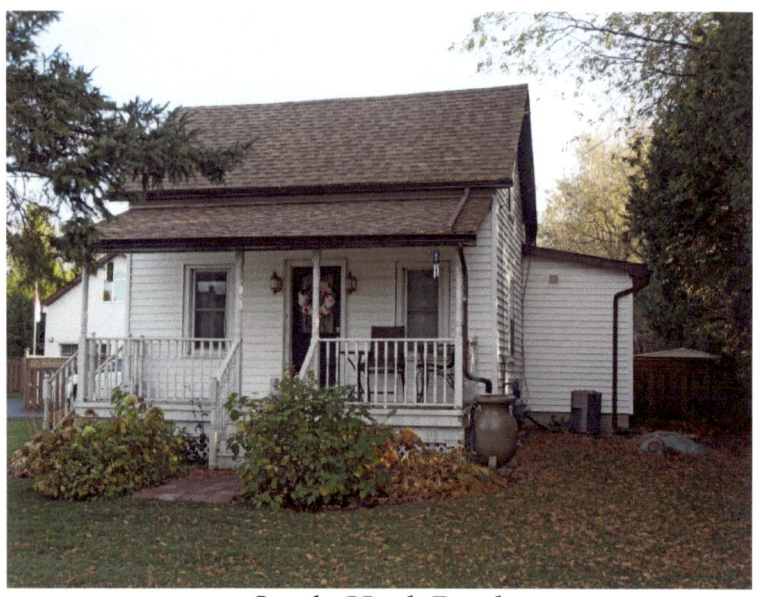

Sandy Hook Road

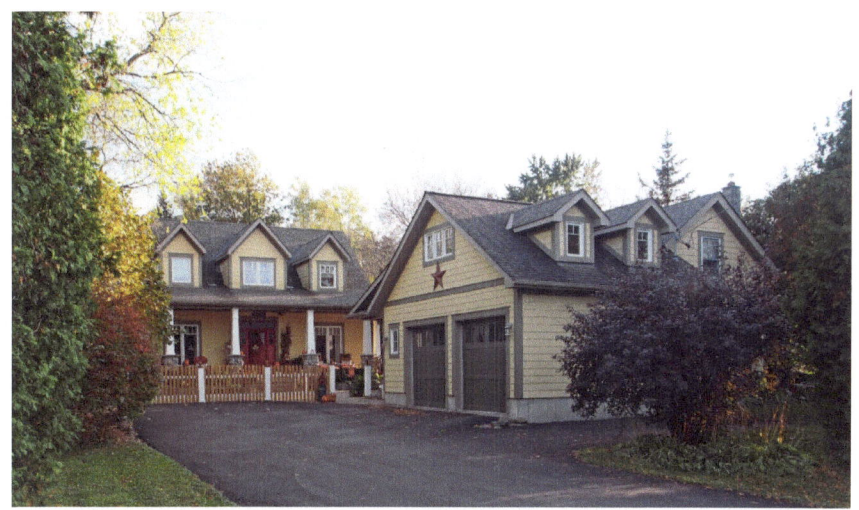

40 Sandy Hook Road - Crosby House - Ira Crosby built a Victorian frame 1½ storey with gable dormers on the sides.

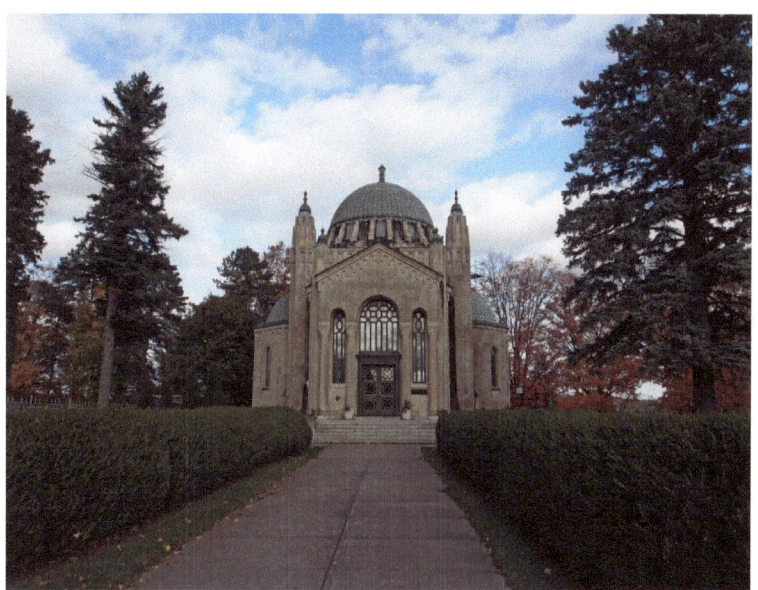

The Thomas Foster Memorial Temple, erected in 1935-36 by the former mayor of Toronto, is situated a short distance north of town. Inspired by Foster's visit to India, the Temple was designed by architects J.H. Craig (1889–1954) and H.H. Madrill (1889–1998).

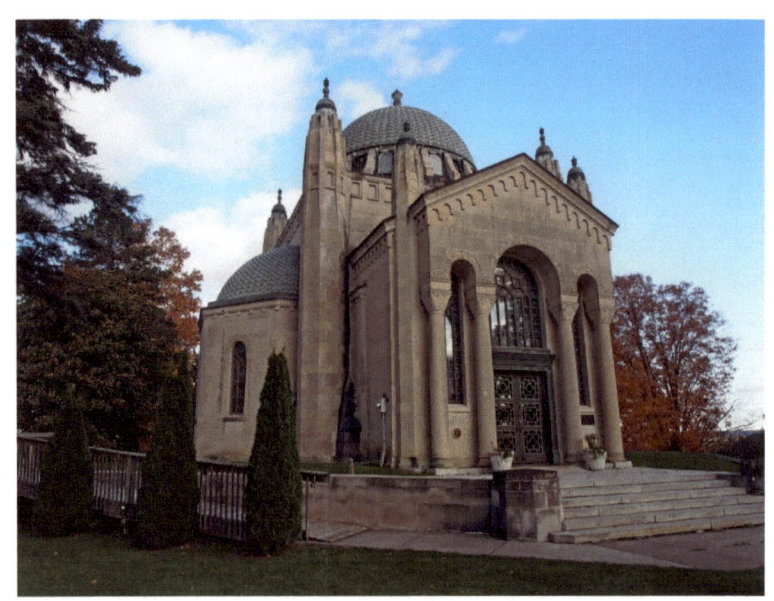

9449 Regional Road 1

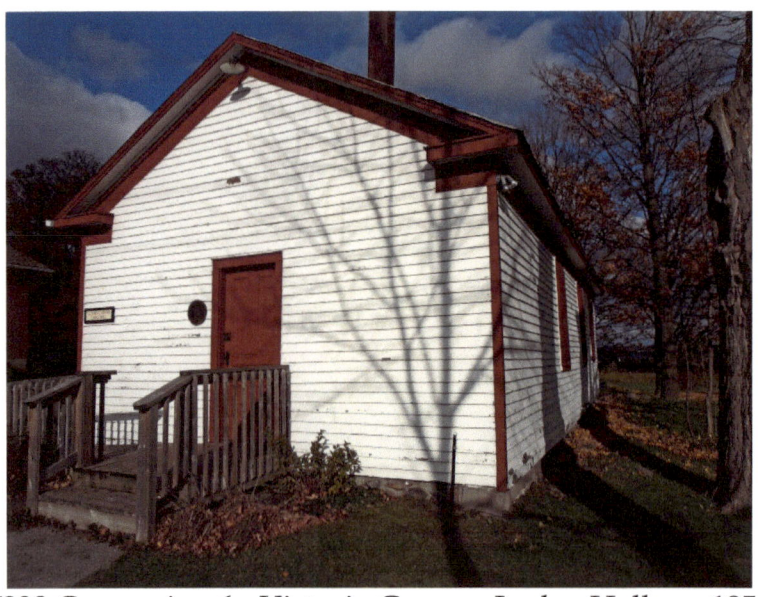

7239 Concession 6 – Victoria Corners Lodge Hall – c. 1856

Uxbridge Historical Centre
7239 Concession 6

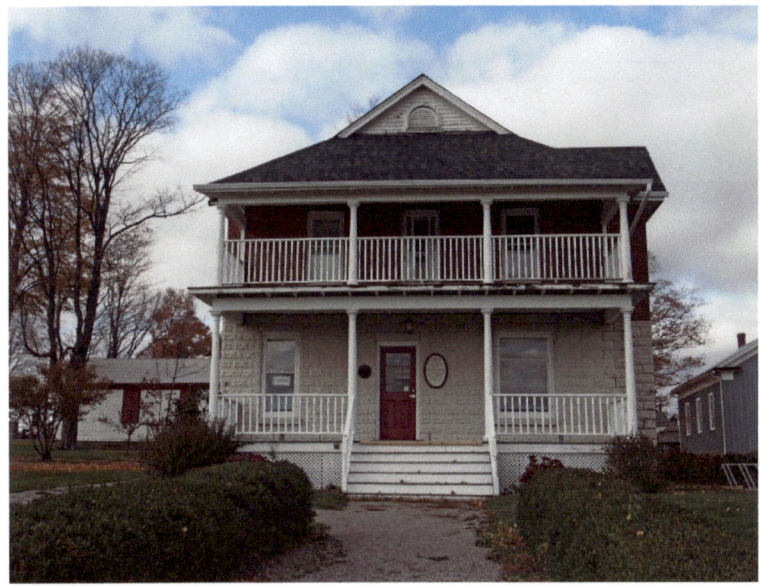

Stokes-Kydd House - Built in 1908 on the east side of Uxbridge, served as a residence for former Councilor Deputy Reeve and Reeve, George Stokes and later was purchased by George and Nellie Kydd. Mrs. Kydd served as the first woman Mayor in Uxbridge in 1963.

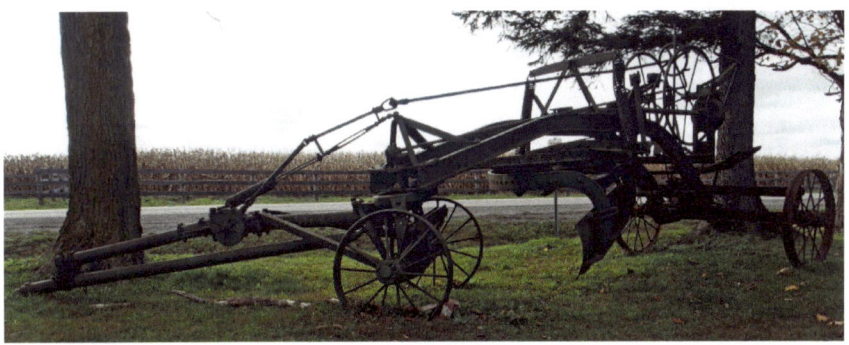

Road grader

7239 Concession 6

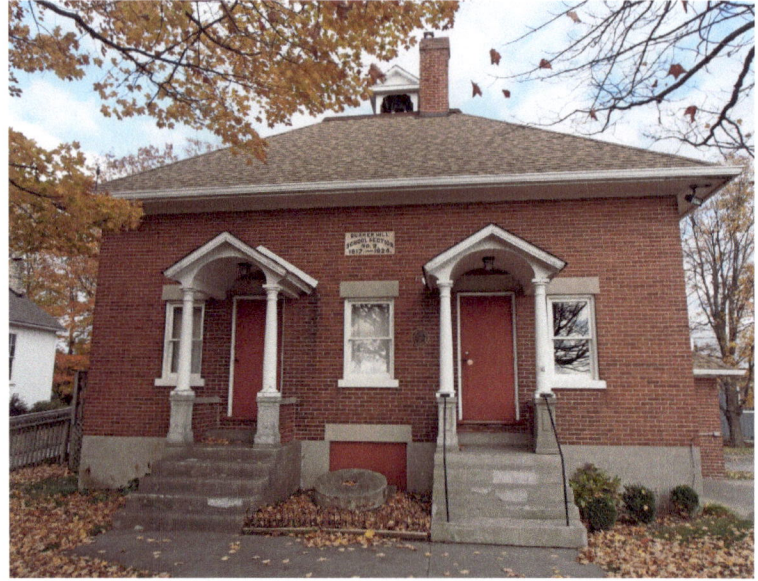

Quaker Hill School S.S. No. 2 – c. 1924

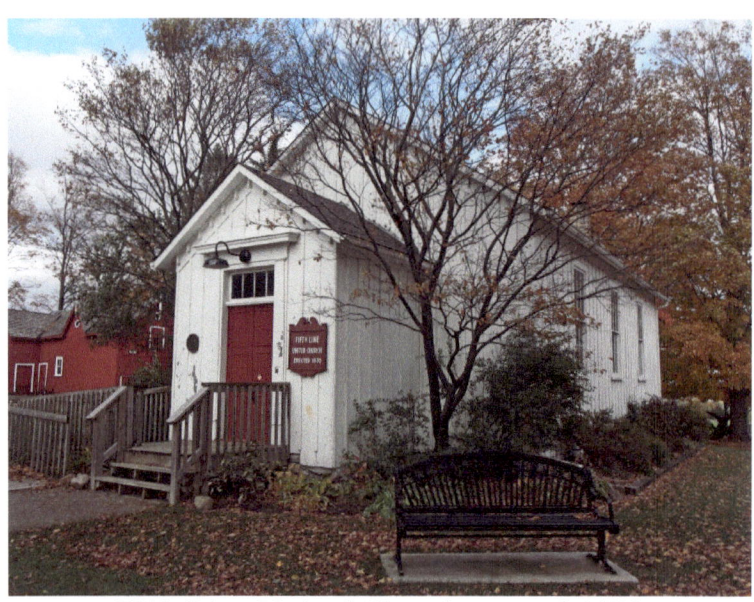

Fifth Line United Church erected 1870

7239 Concession 6

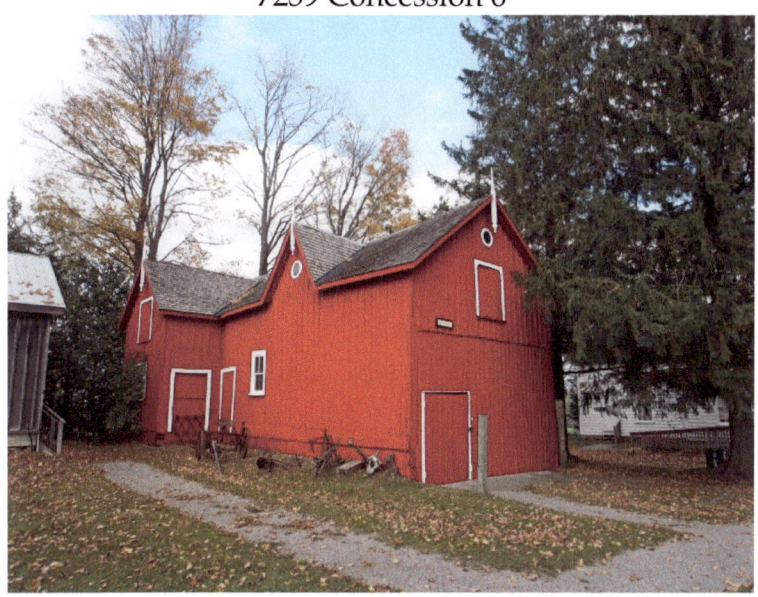

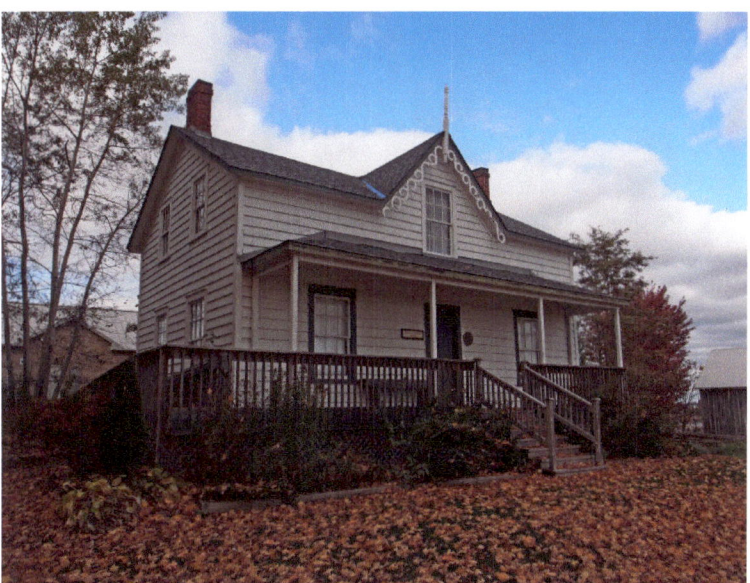

Gould-Carmody House - Built in 1860 by Joseph Gould, the local MPP, this is the original farmhouse on the Gould property where the Historical Centre is now located.

7239 Concession 6

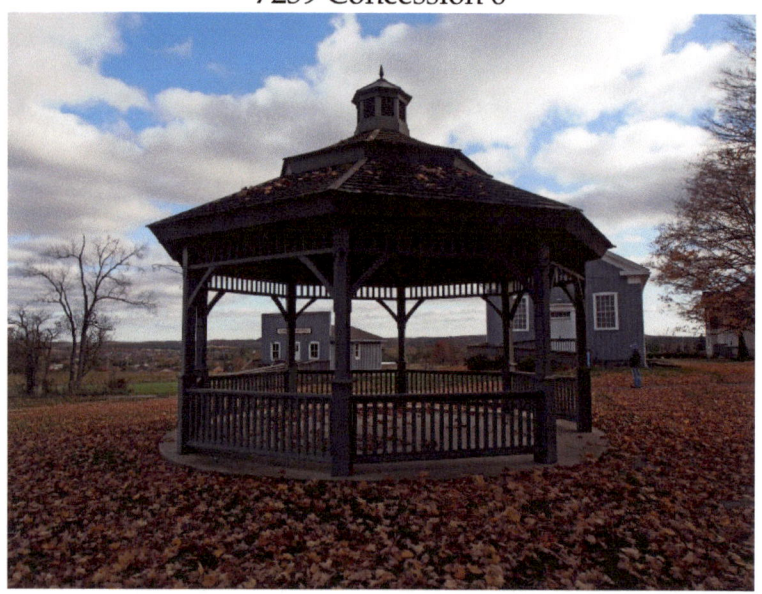

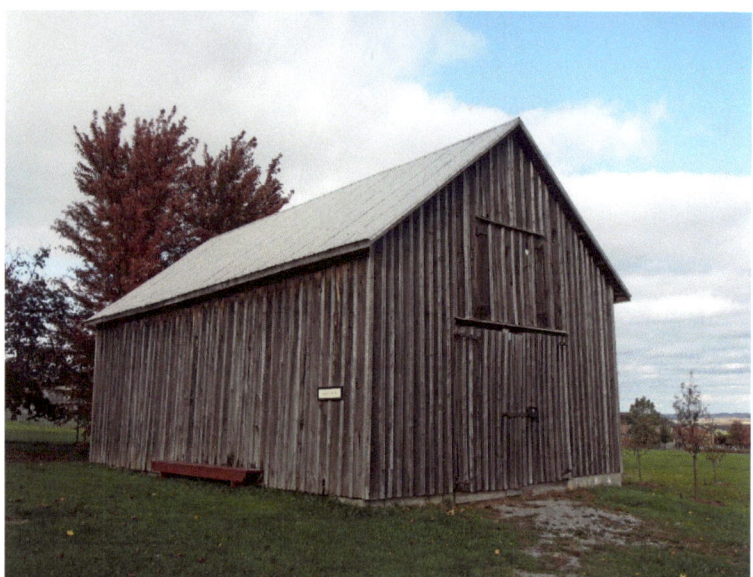

Built in the 1900s, the Nesbitt Shed originally sat on Part of Lot 14, Concession 6 on the property owned by Robert Lewis and Muriel Nesbitt and was used to store a buggy.

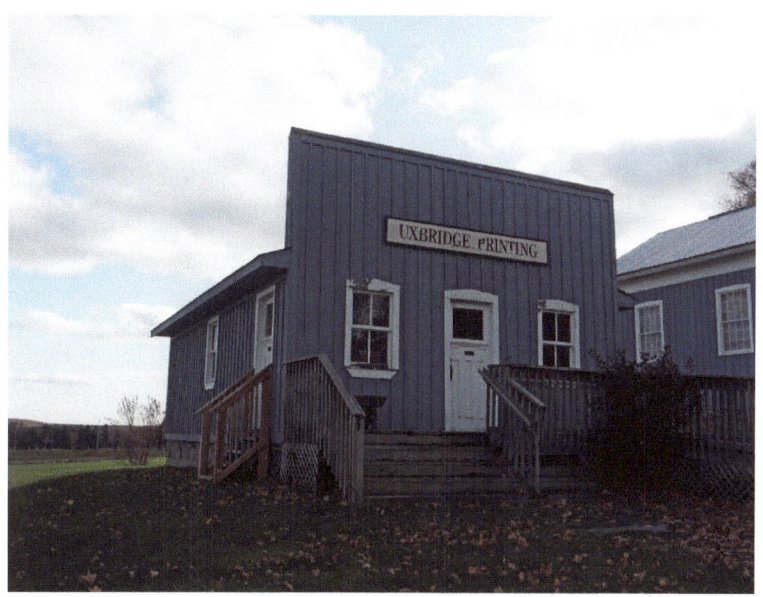

Uxbridge Printing

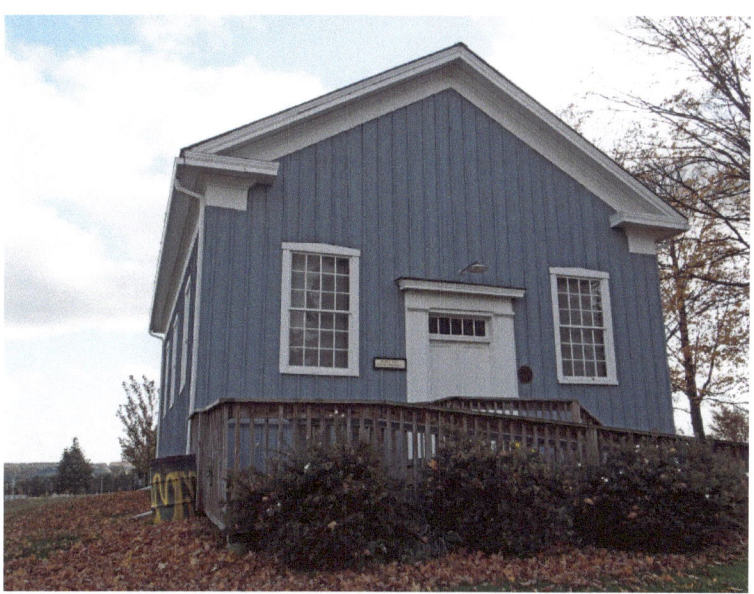

Scott Township Municipal Hall - Built in 1860 on northeast corner of Lot 14, Concession 5, this 'barn farmed' building used by Scott Township Council from 1860-1967.

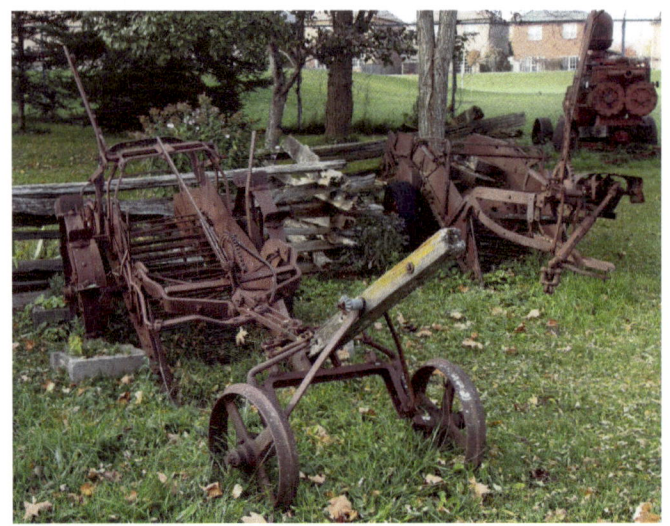
Potato digger

Leaskdale

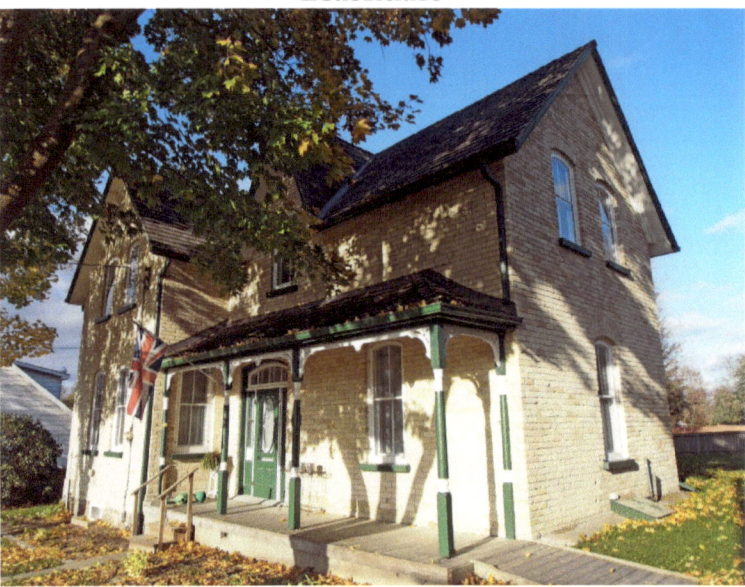

Leaskdale Manse was the former home of author Lucy Maud Montgomery of Anne of Green Gables fame. She lived here from 1911 to 1926, and wrote half of her books at what is now the site of the Leaskdale Manse Museum.

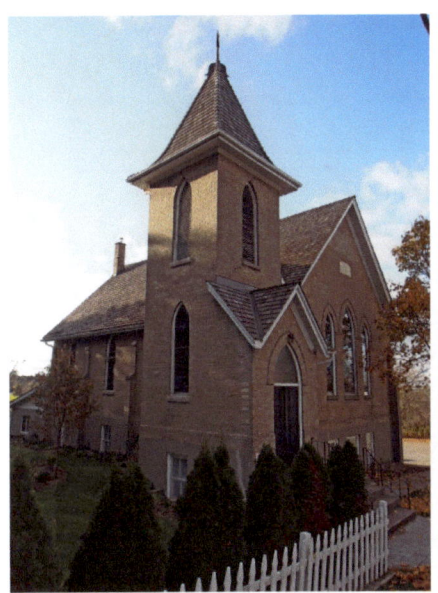 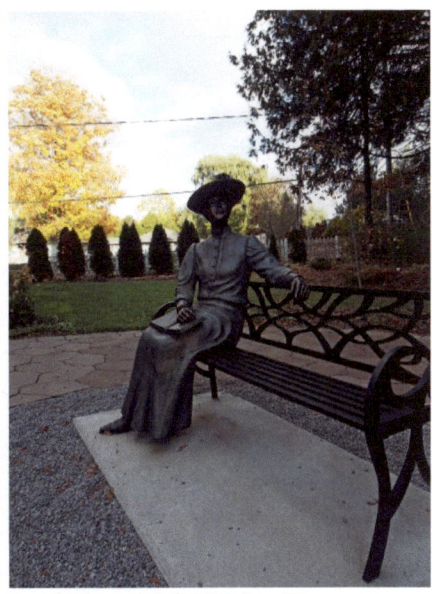

St. Paul's Presbyterian Church erected 1906 – Lucy Montgomery's husband, Rev. Ewan Macdonald, was minister here from 1910-1926.

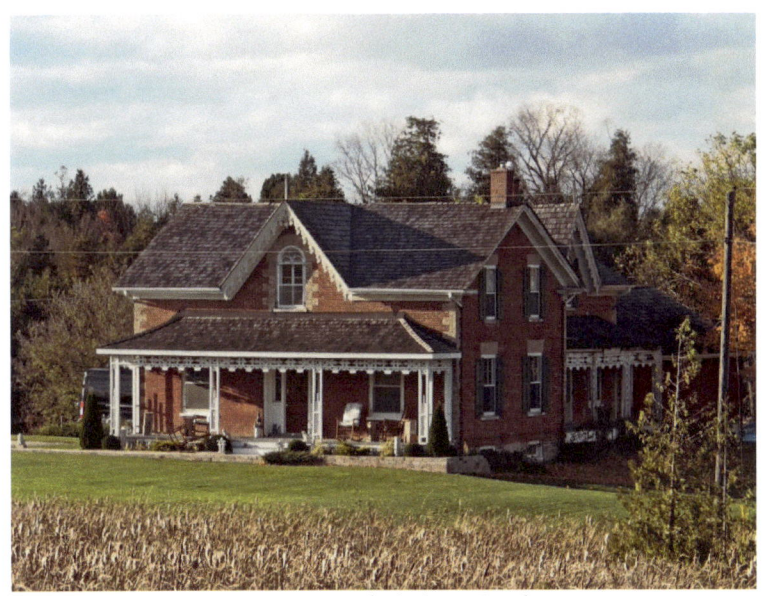

#690 – Leaskdale - Gothic

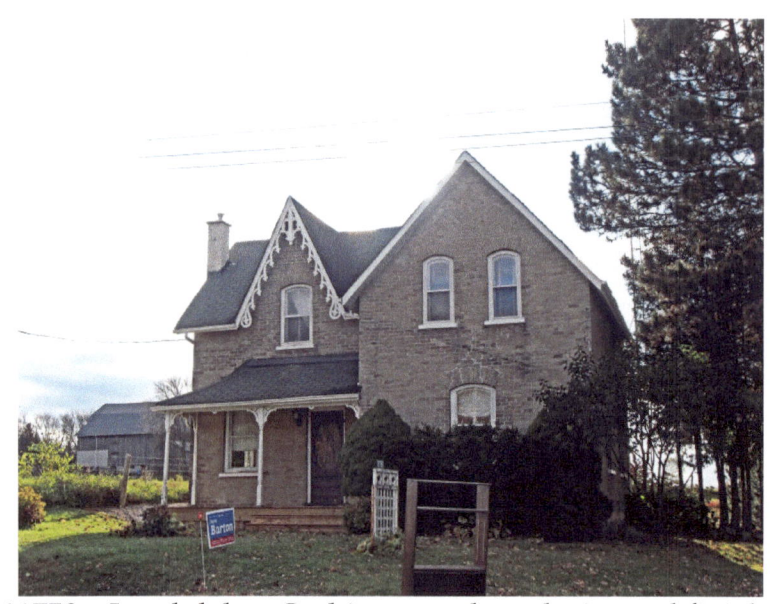

#11750 – Leaskdale – Gothic, verge board trim and finial on gable

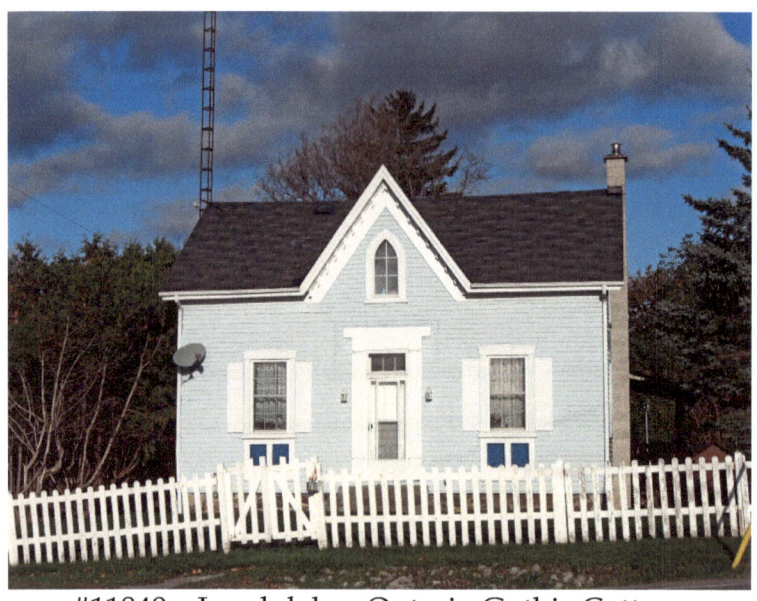

#11849 – Leaskdale – Ontario Gothic Cottage

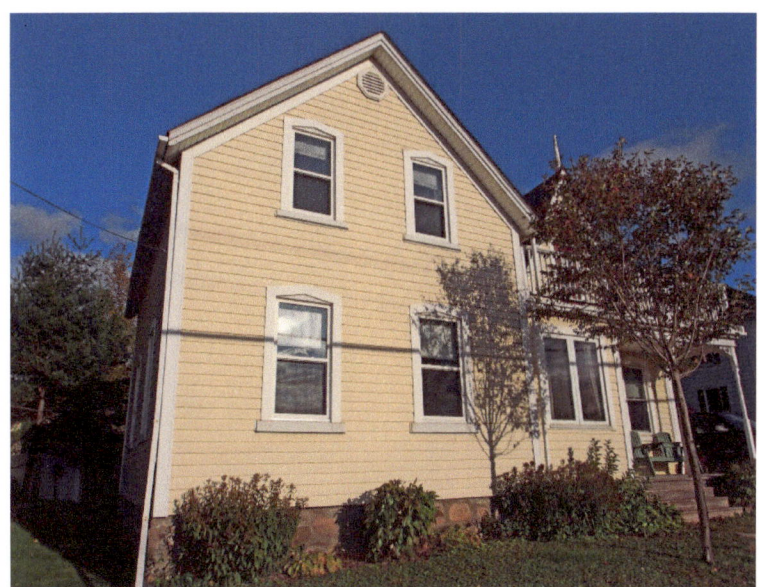

Leaskdale

Goodwood

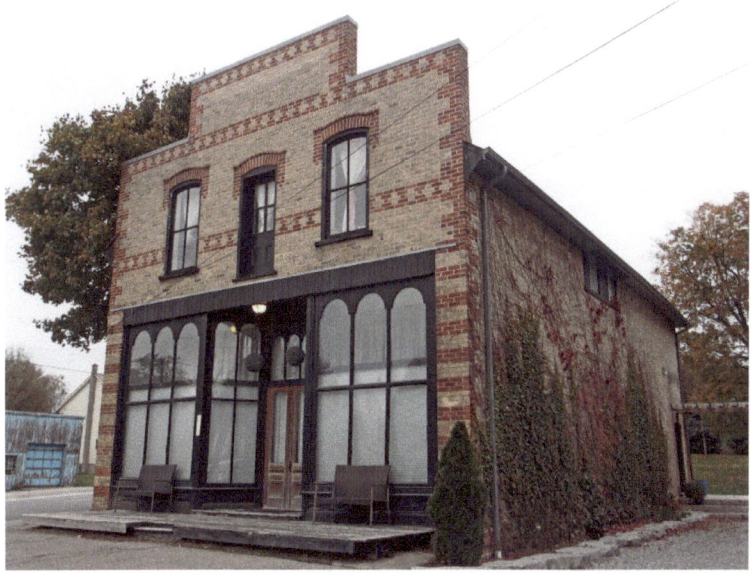

Front Street – stepped parapet, dichromatic brickwork

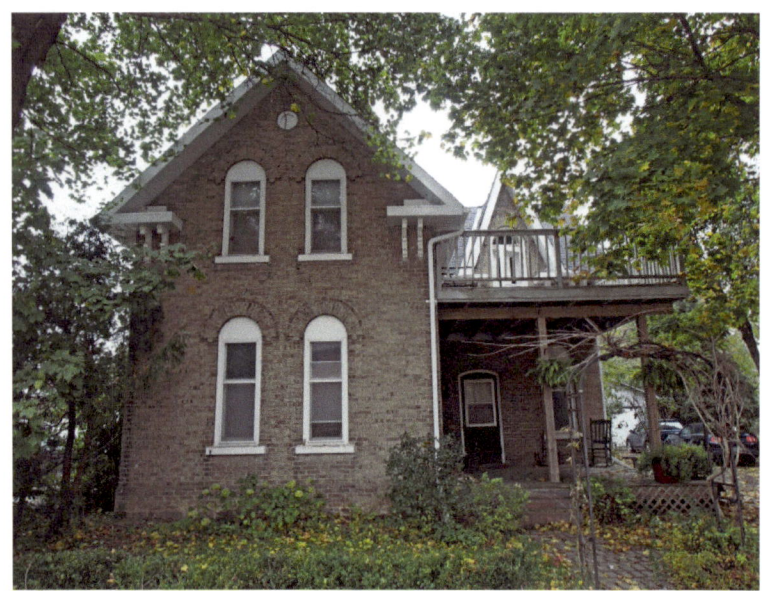

Front Street – cornice return on gable, cornice brackets

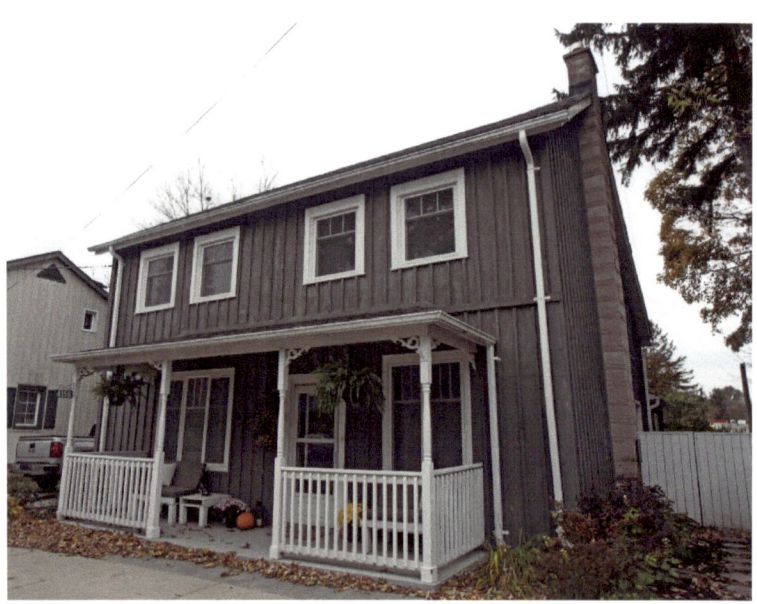

4150 Front Street

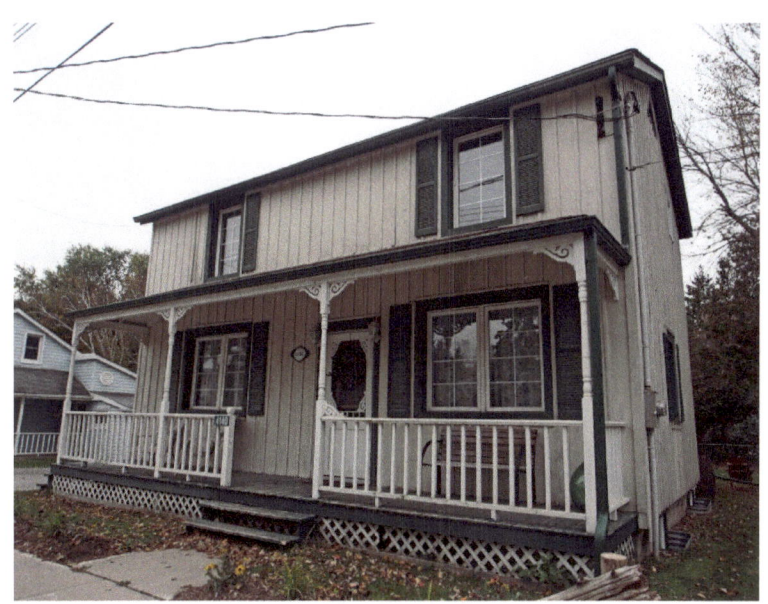

4140 Front Street

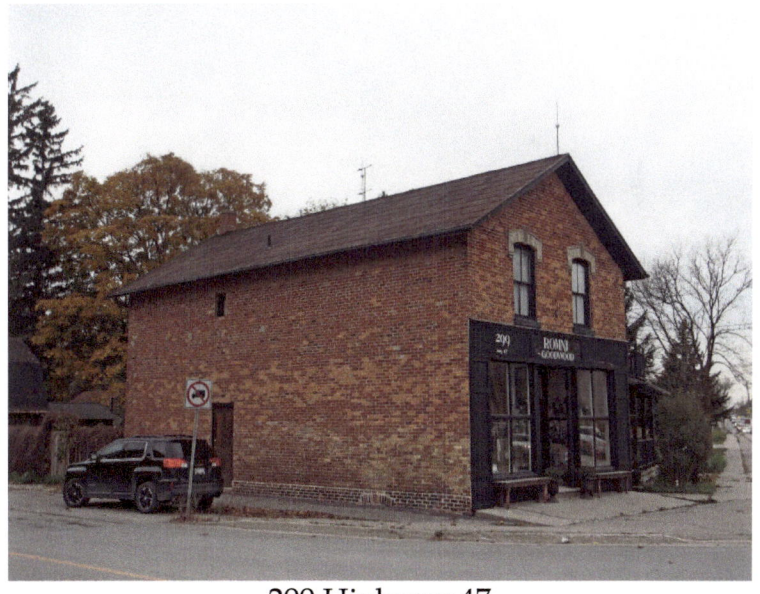

299 Highway 47

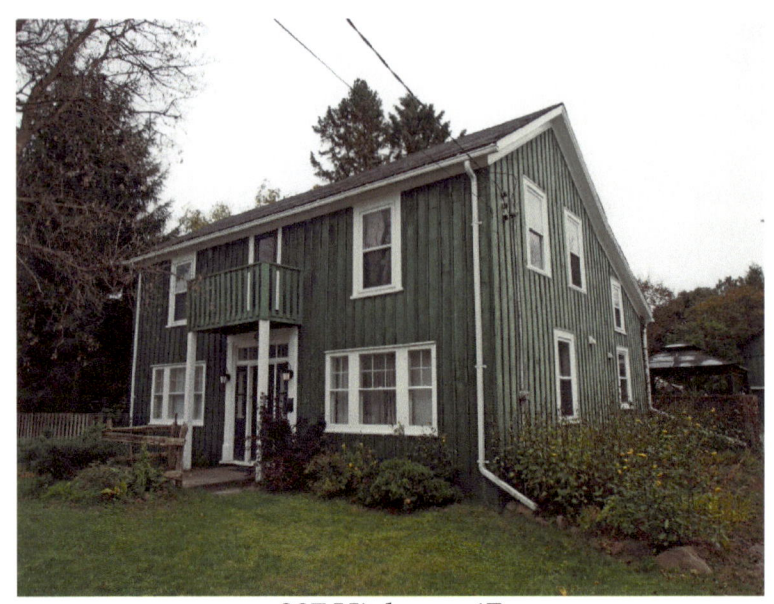

297 Highway 47

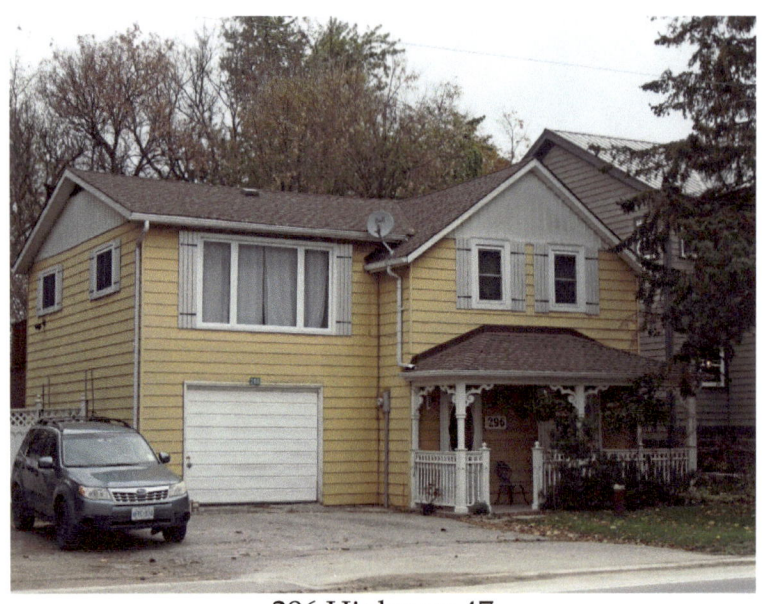

296 Highway 47

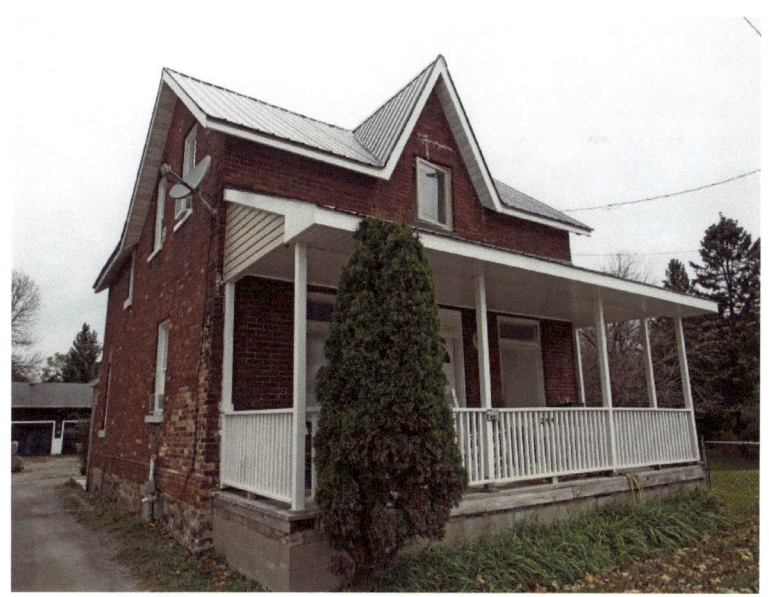

294 Highway 47 – Ontario Gothic Cottage

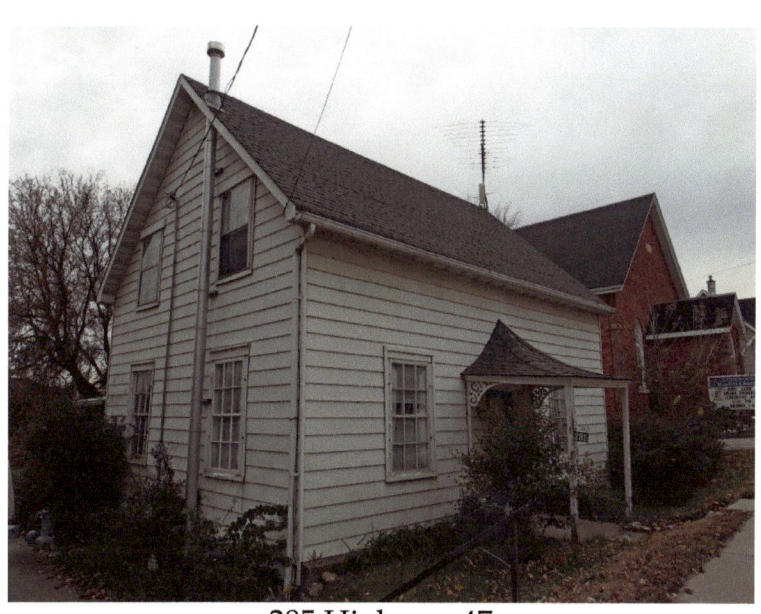

285 Highway 47

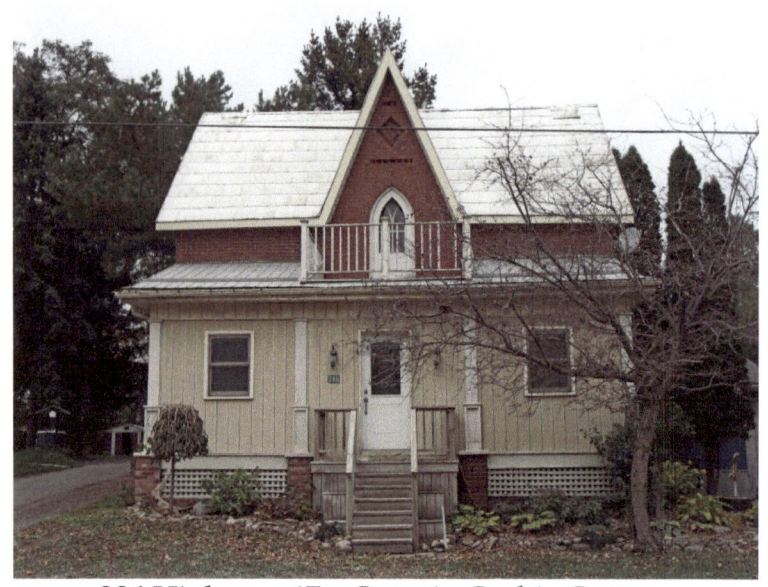

286 Highway 47 – Ontario Gothic Cottage

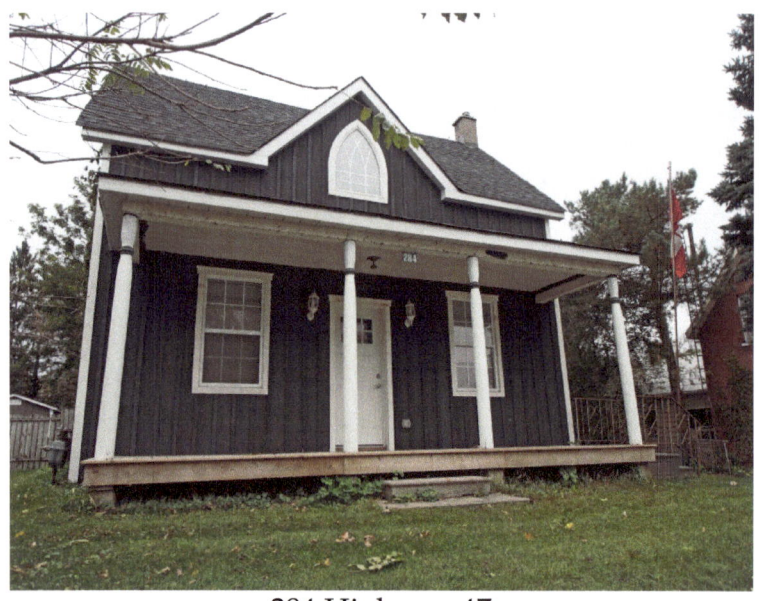

284 Highway 47

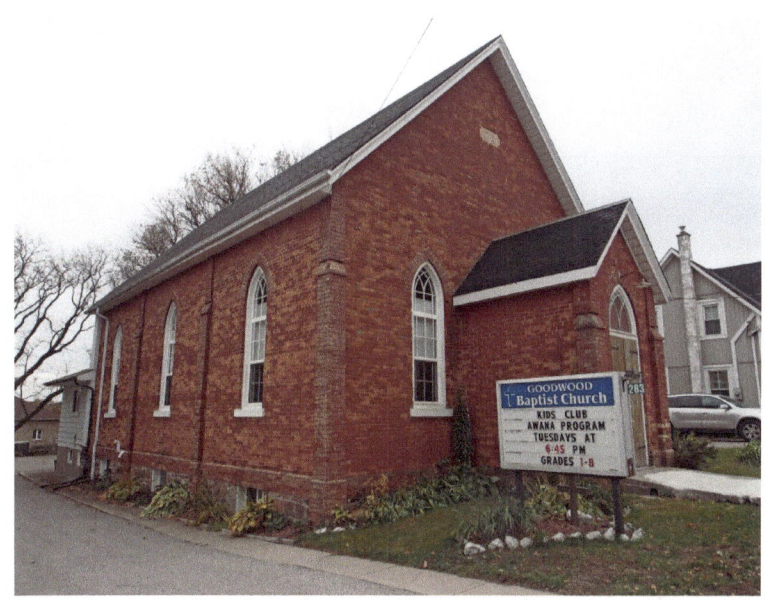

283 Highway 47 – Goodwood Baptist Church – A.D. 1878 – Gothic, lancet windows, buttresses

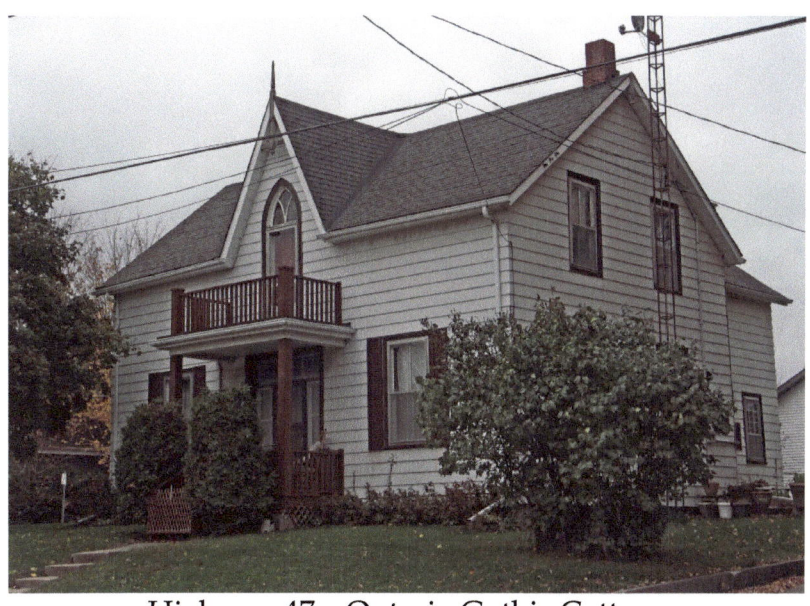

Highway 47 – Ontario Gothic Cottage

Building Styles

Edwardian, 1900-1930 – This style bridges the ornate and elaborate styles of the Victorian era and the simplified styles of the 20th century. Edwardian Classicism provided simple, balanced facades, simple rooflines, dormer windows, large front porches, and smooth brick surfaces. Voussoirs and keystones are used sparingly and are understated. Finials and cresting are absent. Cornice brackets and braces are block-like and openings have flat arches or plain stone lintels.

Georgian, before 1860 – This style began with the British King Georges in the 18th century. These buildings have balanced facades around a central door, medium-pitched gable roofs, and small paned windows.

Gothic Revival, 1830-1890 – These decorative buildings have sharply-pitched gables with highly detailed verge boards, pointed-arch window openings, and dichromatic brickwork. It is a common style in Ontario.

Ontario Cottage - one or one-and-a-half story buildings with a cottage or hip roof. The cottage roof is an equal hip roof where each hip extends to a point in the center of the roof. The hip roof has a long hip in the center. The Ontario Cottage is the vernacular design of the Regency Cottage which generally has a more ornate doorway and a partial or full verandah surrounding it. The roof can have a dormer, a belvedere, and generally two chimneys.

Other Books by Barbara Raue

Coins of Gold
Arrows, Indians and Love
The Life and Times of Barbara
The Cromwell Family Book
Laura Secord Discovered
Daddy Where Are You?

Montana Series
Book 1: Montana Dream
Book 2: Life on the Montana Frontier
Book 3: Montana to Boston and Back
Book 4: Montana Sons Go to War
Book 5: Montana Sons Return from War

Donaldson Series
Book 1: Rite of Passage
Book 2: Rite of Marriage

© 2021 by Barbara Raue - All the photos in this book have been taken with my cameras. I own the rights to them.

Barbara is The Authority on Saving Our History One Photo at a Time. She is pursuing her interest in photography and architecture by preserving a record through photos of old buildings from the 1800s and 1900s with their unique architecture. Enjoy the beautiful architecture in the comfort of your living room. Dream about what it was like in those by-gone days. Dream about what it was like to live in a mansion like one of those in this book.

Barbara Raue, a wife, mother and grandmother, is an avid reader and writer. She has researched and compiled several family histories. In 2010, Barbara published her book "Coins of Gold," which celebrates the courageous life of her mother, May Todd. Barbara's second book is a historical fiction "Arrows, Indians and Love" which takes place in Boonesborough, Kentucky during the time of Daniel Boone. In 2013, Barbara published *The Cromwell Family Book* in which she traces her ancestry generations back into Great Britain. Her second novel is called *Laura Secord Discovered,* in which the story of Laura's service during the War of 1812 is shared. Barbara's memoir is titled *Daddy Where Are You?* It tells of her life growing up without a father. Five novels in the Montana Series have been published, *Montana Dream, Life on the Montana Frontier, Montana to Boston and Back, Montana Sons Go to War,* and *Montana Sons Return from War.* The Donaldson series of two novels is available: *Rite of Passage* and *Rite of Marriage.*

This is a link to Barbara's website to view all of her books
http://barbararaue.ca

www.ingramcontent.com/pod-product-compliance
Lightning Source LLC
Chambersburg PA
CBHW040229220526

45473CB00001B/178